Eat Smart
IN
SICILY

Eat Smart IN SICILY

How to Decipher the Menu
Know the Market Foods
&
Embark on a Tasting Adventure

Joan Peterson and Marcella Croce

Illustrated by Susan Chwae

GINKGO PRESS, INC
Madison, Wisconsin

Eat Smart in Sicily
Joan B. Peterson and Marcella Croce

Map lettering is by Gail L. Carlson; cover and insert photographs are by Joan Peterson; photograph of Joan Peterson by Susan Chwae; photograph of Marcella Croce by Andrea Matranga.

The quote by James A. Michener from "This Great Big Wonderful World," from the March 1956 issue of Travel-Holiday Magazine, © 1956 by James A. Michener, is reprinted by permission of William Morris Agency, LLC, on behalf of the author.

Publisher's Cataloging-in-Publication
(Provided by Quality Books, Inc.)
Peterson, Joan
    Eat smart in Sicily : how to decipher the menu, know the market foods & embark on a tasting adventure / by Joan Peterson and Marcella Croce ; illustrated by Susan Chwae.
    p. cm.
    Includes bibliographical references and index.
    LCCN 2007908347
    ISBN-13: 978-0-9776801-1-5
    ISBN-10: 0-9776801-1-8

    1. Cookery, Italian--Sicilian style. 2. Diet--Italy --Sicily. 3. Food habits--Italy--Sicily. 4. Cookery-- Italy--Sicily. 5. Sicily (Italy)--Guidebooks. 6. Sicily (Italy)--Description and travel. I. Croce, Marcella, 1949- II. Title.

TX723.2.S55P48 2008   641.5945'8
                    QBI08-600075
Printed in the United States of America

To Giovanni Matranga

His love and knowledge of Sicilian food
added savor to every page.

Contents

Preface   *ix*
Acknowledgments   *xi*

The Cuisine of Sicily   1

An historical survey of the development of Sicily's cuisine.

Early Civilizations   1
The Greeks   3
The Romans   4
The Vandals, Goths and Byzantines   6
The Arabs   7
The Norman French   10
Other Europeans   12
   Hohenstaufen   12
   French Angevin   13
   Royal House of Aragon   13
   The Spanish   14
   Royal House of Bourbon   15
Italian Unification   16

Local Sicilian Food   19

A quick tour of Sicilian foods and their local variations.

Sicilian Food in a Nutshell   19
The Provinces of Sicily   31
   Western Sicily   32
   Central Sicily   35
   Eastern Sicily   36
   Southeastern Sicily   38

Tastes of Sicily   41

A selection of delicious, easy-to-prepare recipes to try before leaving home.

Shopping in Sicily's Food Markets 71

Tips to increase your savvy in both the exciting outdoor food markets and modern supermarkets.

Resources 73

A listing of stores carrying Sicilian foods and groups offering opportunities for person-to-person contact through home visits to gain a deeper understanding of the country, including its cuisine.

Online Suppliers of Sicilian Foods 73
Tours and Travel Advice 74
Some Useful Organizations to Know About 75

Helpful Phrases 77

Phrases in English translated to Italian, with additional phonetic interpretation, which will assist you in finding, ordering and buying foods or ingredients.

Phrases for Use in Restaurants 77
Phrases for Use in Food Markets 79
Other Useful Phrases 80

Menu Guide 81

An extensive listing of menu entries in Italian (and some Sicilian), with English translations, to make ordering food an easy and immediately rewarding experience.

Foods and Flavors Guide 109

A comprehensive glossary of ingredients, kitchen utensils and cooking methods in Italian (and some Sicilian), with English translations.

Restaurants 137

Chefs who taught us much about Sicilian food.

Bibliography 139
Index 141

Preface

> If you reject the food, ignore the customs, fear the
> religion and avoid the people, you might better
> stay home. You are like a pebble thrown into
> water; you become wet on the surface but you are
> never a part of the water.
>
> —JAMES A. MICHENER

I strongly feel that the best way to know a culture is through its foodways. What could be more satisfying than getting immersed in a new culture by mingling with local people in the places where they enjoy good food and conversation—in their favorite neighborhood cafés, restaurants, picnic spots or outdoor markets? When traveling I try to capture the essence of a country through its food, and seek out unfamiliar ingredients and preparations that provide new tastes. By meandering on foot or navigating on local buses, I have discovered serendipitously many memorable eateries away from more heavily trafficked tourist areas.

The purpose of the EAT SMART guides is to provide information for travelers that will empower and encourage them to sample new and often unusual foods, and will allow them to discover new ways of preparing or combining familiar ingredients. I know informed travelers will be more open to experimentation. The EAT SMART guides also will help steer the traveler away from the foods they wish to avoid—everyone confesses to disliking something!

This guide has four main chapters. The first provides a history of Sicilian cuisine. It is followed by a chapter with descriptions of local Sicilian foods. The other main chapters are extensive listings, placed near the end of the book for easy reference. The *Menu Guide* is an alphabetical compilation of menu entries, including local specialities in addition to general Sicilian fare. Some not-to-be-missed dishes with island-wide popularity are labeled "Sicilian classic" in the margin next to the menu entry. Some favorite local dishes of Sicily—also not to be missed—are labeled "local favorites." The *Foods & Flavors Guide* contains a translation of food items and terms associated with preparing and serving food. This glossary will be useful in interpreting menus, since it is impractical to cover in the *Menu Guide* all the flavors or combinations possible for certain dishes.

Also included in the book is a chapter offering hints on browsing and shopping in the food markets and one with phrases that will be useful in restaurants and food markets to learn more about the foods of Sicily. A chapter is devoted to classic and nouvelle Sicilian recipes. Do take time to experiment with these recipes before departure; it is a wonderful and immediately rewarding way to preview Sicilian food. Most special Sicilian ingredients in these recipes can be obtained in the United States; substitutions for unavailable ingredients are given. Sources of hard-to-find Sicilian ingredients can be found in the *Resources* chapter, which also cites groups that offer the opportunity to have person-to-person contact through home visits to gain a deeper understanding of the country, including its cuisine.

I am very pleased to introduce Marcella Croce, co-author of this travel guidebook. Marcella was born in Palermo and is a journalist and author. Her extensive knowledge of the rich culinary heritage of her native Sicily has been invaluable to this project.

Buon viaggio and buon appetito!

JOAN PETERSON
Madison, Wisconsin

Acknowledgments

We gratefully acknowledge those who assisted us in preparing this book. Thanks to Susan Chwae (Ginkgo Press) for illustrations, cover design and photograph of author Joan Peterson; Andrea Matranga for photograph of author Marcella Croce; Gail Carlson for enlivening our maps with her handwriting; and Nicol Knappen (Ekeby) for book design.

For contributing recipes and/or providing cooking demonstrations or winery tours, we thank the chefs who are mentioned elsewhere (see *Restaurants,* p. 137) as well as the following chefs, food and wine professionals, "home cooks" and authors in Sicily: Annamaria Simili, Azienda Agricola Trinità, Mascalucia; Wiebke Petersen, Tenuta di Donnafugata, Marsala; Massimo Floridia, B&B Cavour il Conte Camillo, Palermo; Maria Teresa Allegra, Casa Migliaca, Pettineo; Chiara Agnello, Azienda Agricola Fattoria Mosé, Agrigento; Marilena Leta, Cantine Florio, Marsala; Maria Grammatico, La Pasticceria di Maria Grammatico, Erice; Anna Tasca Lanza, Regaleali, Vallelunga; Wanda and Giovanna Tornabene, Tenuta Gangivecchio, Gangi; Giusy Costanzo, Corrado Costanzo Pasticceria and Gelateria, Noto; Mary Taylor Simeti, Alcamo; Giovanni Matranga, Palermo; and in the United States (Wisconsin): Dr. Giovanna Miceli-Jeffries, Conchera Capadona, Catherine Tripalin Murray, and Matt Pratt, RP's Fork & Spoon Café, all from Madison.

We are indebted to many people for introducing us to local foods, for help in identifying local Sicilian foods and menu items, for providing resource materials, for taste testing recipes, or for guide and tourist services. In Sicily, thanks to Barbara Muratore and Nino Barcia, Agriturismo Antica Stazione Ferroviaria, Ficuzza; Piero Buffa, Baglio di Pianetto, San Cristina Gela; Davide Zuccaro, Salumificio San Cero, Marineo; Stefano Plescia, Bar Elena, Piana degli Albanesi; Mimma and Mercurio Carbone, Piana degli Albanesi; Pasquale Tornatore, Slow Food Movement, Caltanissetta; Francesco Daina,

Caltanissetta; Leonardo Gaglio, Montelepre; Gaetano Pennino, Director, Casa Museo Antonino Uccello, Palazzolo Acreide; Rosario Acquaviva, Director Museo Civiltà Contadina, Buscemi; Rita Li Calzi, Agrigento; Carmelo Galvagno, Catania; Maria Crivello, Palermo; Itria Corsini, Pasticceria Corsini, Palazzolo Acreide; Maria Rosa Ruggeri, Taormina; Franco Saccà, Slow Food Movement, Trapani; Giovannella Brancato, Pantelleria; Fabrizio Carrera, Director of the Italian online magazine *Cronache di gusto* (www.cronachedigusto.it), Palermo; Giuseppe Barbera, Professor of Horticulture, University of Palermo; Michele Monti, Professor of Agriculture, University of Reggio Calabria; Silvano Riggio, Professor of Marine Biology, University of Palermo; Tina Genovese, Turin; Chiara Agnello, Azienda Agricola Fattoria Mosé, Agrigento; Dott. Agr. Paolo Girgenti, director of the Menfi branch of the Department of Agriculture and Forestry; Giovanna Palermo, Sciacca. In Greece, thanks to Christos Kronis. In the United States, thanks to Dr. Giovanna Miceli-Jeffries, Department of French and Italian, University of Wisconsin–Madison; Shinji Muramoto, Restaurant Muramoto; Riccardo Bambi, Suite Retreats; Catherine Tripalin Murray, Greenbush...remembered; Teresa Pullara, Bunky's Cafe; Patty Werner, Alfonso Gutierrez, Ruth and Robert Martin, Judy Allen, Bea and Leon Lindberg, all in Madison, Wisconsin; John and Dorothy Priske, Fountain Prairie Inn and Farms, Fall River, Wisconsin; Ruby and Joe Cabibbo, Cabibbo's Bakery, Stoughton, Wisconsin; Marilyn and Don Dralle, CC Angus Beef, Mineral Point, Wisconsin; Jeffrey and Stacy Bartelt, Phoenix, Arizona; Donna Maroni, Chapel Hill, North Carolina; Catherine Lambrecht, Chicago.

We gratefully acknowledge the expert assistance of Jessica Baldone, Borzì Travel Agency, Palermo, for an itinerary that filled our needs perfectly.

And special thanks to Brook Soltvedt, a most perceptive and helpful editor.

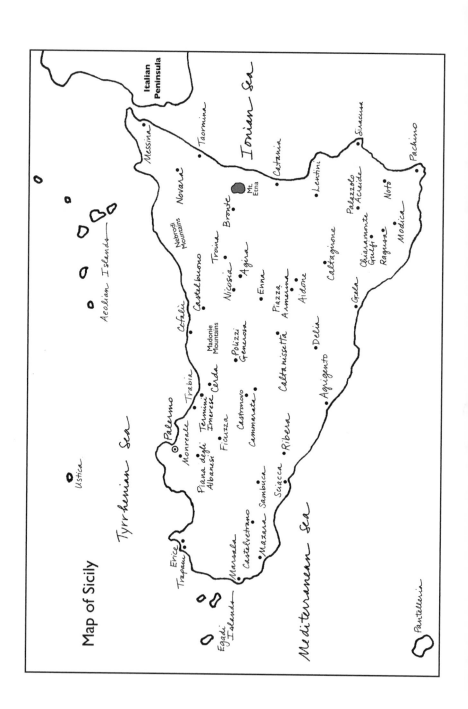

Map of Sicily

The Cuisine of Sicily

An Historical Survey

Sicily is the largest and most significant Mediterranean island. Its triangular shape prompted the Greeks to dub it *Trinacria,* meaning triangle, but its modern name was contributed by ancient inhabitants, the *Siculi* (Sicels). Sicily is also the largest region of Italy and has within its administrative domain an archipelago of lesser islands: the seven islands of the Aeolian group north of Milazzo; Ustica, north of Palermo; the three Egadi islands west of Trapani; Pantelleria, southwest of Sicily and the three remote Pelagie islands south of Sicily, one of which is the southernmost point of Italy.

The remarkably variegated and beautiful landscape of Sicily is made up of hilly uplands interspersed with fertile valleys, and is edged in the south and west by fertile coastal strips. In the mountainous north, Mt. Etna, Europe's largest active volcano, is an almost 11,000-foot sentinel, dominating the northeast and much of central Sicily. Etna's periodic eruptions fertilize the soil with nutrient-rich volcanic ash, and a great many crops flourish on her foothills. Rich soils and a temperate climate of mild, moderately rainy winters and hot, dry summers favored agriculture from the beginning of history.

The island's size and strategic location at the crossroads of trade in the Mediterranean—about 2 miles from the Italian mainland and about 90 miles from Africa—made it the center of the Western world for centuries. This, coupled with an abundance of natural resources, all but ensured a history of a succession of foreign colonizers, who collectively provided a culinary identity quite different from the rest of Italy.

Early Civilizations

The earliest known agricultural society in Sicily was the Neolithic Stentinello culture, so named because it was first identified in the village of Stentinello

1

near Syracuse in the southeastern part of the island. The culture dated to the 5th and 4th millennia BCE. Its origin is unclear.

Three successive waves of ancient colonization appear in the archaeological record between the 2nd and 1st millennia BCE. The earliest group, the *Sicani* (Sicans), may have migrated from northern Africa via Spain, and settled in western Sicily. They were followed by the *Siculi* (Sicels), who are thought to have crossed the Strait of Messina from the Italian mainland. They inhabited the eastern and southeastern coastal areas. The origin of the third group, the *Elimi* (Elymians) is even less certain. They settled in the northwestern part of the island. Their principal cities were Segesta and Erice, the hilltop town on the west coast. All of these ancient cultures of Sicily are frequently referred to as indigenous peoples.

The ancient farmers lived in huts in often fortified villages. Some also used caves as shelters. They cultivated crops of wheat, lentils, barley, fava beans, peas, figs and almonds. The primitive varieties of wheat they grew—einkorn and emmer—had hulls that had to be parched, or heated, to release the grain. Later in the prehistoric period, the more-easily milled soft-hulled or "naked" wheats would predominate. Large, flat grinding stones, or querns, were used to grind the grain, which was stored in clay-lined ditches or in ceramic vessels. As sheep, goats, cattle, pigs and dogs were domesticated, deer and wild boars became less important as food sources. Fish, also a basic food commodity, were caught by nets and hooks, and large quantities of shellfish were consumed. Drawings of tuna as early as the Mesolithic Era have been found on cave walls in the Egadi Islands (Levanzo). Tuna still is a very important menu item in Sicily today.

Archaeological evidence reveals that ceramic crocks were used to boil foods such as legumes and grains at household hearths, and grinding stones turned legumes and grains into flour for primitive bread that could be

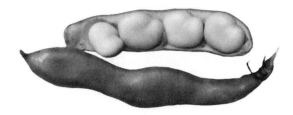

Fava beans (*Vicia faba*), both fresh and dried, are a staple in traditional Sicilian cuisine.

hearth-baked. Pit cooking was utilized as well. Ancient dwelling sites have shallow, earthen pits containing charcoal and fire-blackened stones. The Phoenicians began colonizing Sicily about 800 BCE. This primarily seafaring and trading culture lived on the easternmost shore of the Mediterranean in present-day Lebanon. For several centuries they had traded at coastal villages across the entire Mediterranean before establishing permanent mercantile enclaves in several locations. These included Carthage on the northern coast of Africa and commercial towns primarily in the western part of Sicily: Marsala, Solunto and Palermo, which became the most important Phoenician settlement on the island. They also inhabited the small island of Mozia, situated in a shallow lagoon off Marsala on the western shore, and the island of Pantelleria, located about 68 miles southwest of Sicily. The Phoenicians had saltworks near Mozia that are still in operation today. In 480 BCE the Phoenicians were overpowered by the Greeks in the Battle of Himera, a Greek city on the northern coast of Sicily. This battle marked the beginning of Greek supremacy on the island. A large portion of western Sicily, however, remained under the Phoenicians.

The Greeks

The first colonizers to have a lasting influence in Sicily were the Greeks. Their presence was noted around 800 BCE, concurrent with the arrival of the Phoenicians. They assimilated the indigenous inhabitants and formed their first settlements in eastern coastal regions closest to Greece. The town of Naxos, near Taormina, was founded in 734 BCE, followed by Messina, Syracuse, Lentini, Catania and Megara Hyblaea on the eastern coast; Gela, on the southern coast; Selinunte, Agrigento and Mazara on the western coast; and Termini Imerese on the northern coast. The Greeks' greatest colony in Sicily was Syracuse, which rivaled Athens in prestige and power. The Greeks added many more settlements, both new colonies and Hellenized native colonies, many of which became quite prosperous.

Unlike the Phoenicians, primarily traders uninterested in territorial expansion, the Greeks sought complete colonization of the island. They introduced more advanced agricultural methods and added vegetables, fruits and fowl (hens, ducks, geese, guinea fowl and pigeons) to the larder. Crops of barley, wheat and millet were cultivated. Olive groves and vineyards were established to provide olive oil and wine, essential components of the Greek diet, and extensive bee-keeping operations were established.

The Greeks also brought their knowledge of stock breeding to Sicily. Sheep were especially important for cheese production. Extensive tracts of pasture provided abundant grazing for their animals. Unfortunately, the land was often acquired at the expense of forests, which were denuded for their timber. Ancient Greece had consumed its own forests and there was a great demand for lumber, especially for shipbuilding.

Greek Sicilian gastronomy established a name for itself early on. The term "Syracusan table" appeared in literature and became synonymous with lavish dining. Sicilian food, drink and banqueting customs spread throughout the classical world, hastened somewhat by Sicilian culinary treatises in prose and poetry. In the late 5th century BCE the Sicilian cook Mithaikos detailed food and food preparation in what is considered the first cookbook in Greek. Herakleides of Syracuse, another epicure, wrote his notable cookbook in the 4th century BCE. Around 350 BCE an apparently wealthy and well-traveled Greek, Archestratus of Syracuse, wrote a gastronomic poem, believed to be entitled *Hedupatheia,* or *The Life of Pleasure.* The poem, in the style of a guidebook, describes where to obtain fine foods—especially fish—in Mediterranean coastal cities, and provides detailed instructions for preparing and serving foods. Cooking and serving instructions were elaborately detailed. The hedonism of the poem was tempered by the insistence on culinary simplicity when preparing high-quality foods, said to require little embellishment for pleasuring the palate. To smother them in elaborate sauces would be vulgar and expose one's lack of refinement.

Although the Greeks decisively beat the Phoenicians in 480 BCE, hostilities between the Greeks and the Carthaginians from North Africa (descendents of the Phoenicians) continued for some time afterwards. Greek dominance in Sicily lasted until 212 BCE, when the Romans, who had emerged as a power beginning in the 4th century BCE, sacked Syracuse.

The Romans

The Roman victory in Sicily marked the acquisition of the first Roman province, a significant coup for Rome. Sicily's wheat-growing capacity was well-known and her wheat had been coveted by Rome to feed its burgeoning population and provide field rations for its legions of soldiers. A major dietary staple, wheat was coarsely ground and typically consumed as porridge or thick gruel (*puls* in Latin), or as coarse bread. The Romans expropriated the land and redistributed it as large feudal estates (*latifundia*), some of which remained undivided until the 20th century, a condition that hindered the economic development of Sicily. The *latifundia* overwhelmingly grew wheat, which required minimal attention and favored absentee ownership. Estates often were given as favors to wealthy patrons, usually senatorial families in Rome, who never set foot on the island. The fields were cultivated by Greek Sicilian peasants and by slaves taken in Roman conquests. Smaller parcels of land cultivated by Roman homesteaders grew legumes, vegetables and fruits in addition to wheat. Common field beans—fava beans (*Vicia faba*)—were made into a porridge called *puls fabata* or *fabacia*. *Puls fabata* may be a distant relative of the Sicilian dish *maccu*, a dried fava bean purée or thick soup. A recipe for *maccu* is on p. 46.

Roman cookery had little impact on Greek Sicilian cuisine. If anything, Greek Sicilian cuisine embellished that of Rome. Comparatively few Romans lived and worked on the island, so Sicily under the Romans remained culturally Greek. For an appreciation of the state of culinary arts in the rest of the Roman Empire, there is a marvelously detailed first century compendium, *The Roman Cookery of Apicius,* (*De Re Coquinaria* in Latin), written for the epicurean by M. Gavius Apicius. Its 10 chapters are organized by food groups and together contain about 500 recipes providing insight into the extravagant and gluttonous eating habits of the Roman Empire's upper classes. To satisfy the jaded palate of the elite, condiments and sauces became extremely important, and costly spices were imported from distant foreign lands.

One ingredient known to even earlier cultures was ubiquitous in Roman cookery. Most dishes—even sweets—called for the malodorous, yet tremendously popular, fermented fish paste *garum,* made from the innards of mackerel or tuna. The fish parts were salted and left in large basins in the sun for several months. *Garum* was the liquid in the basins when fermentation was complete. The remaining residue, *allec,* was sold in the markets to the poor. *Garum* production and trade were lucrative from Phoenician to Roman times. Today's traveler can view the remains of basins that date back to the Hellenistic period at the Vendicari Nature

Ancient ceramic amphora used to store and transport fermented fish paste called *garum*.

Reserve near Syracuse and on Isola delle Femmine, an island near the city of the same name, not far from Palermo.

The Roman Empire began to decline in the 2nd century. The Roman presence in Sicily had remained fairly stable up to this time and was comprised of homesteaders, some of the owners of the *latifundia* and the bureaucracy necessary to govern the island. Essentially no Roman building projects were erected on the island; road construction was just sufficient to facilitate grain shipment to the rivers and sea. In the waning days of the Roman Empire, traffic to Sicily began to pick up. Aristocrats from Rome acquired land and built elaborate country lodges and villas as retreats. The floor mosaics of one of these, the Villa Romana del Casale near Piazza Armerina, remain among the most beautiful in the world.

Both Greeks and Romans tolerated the diverse religious sects prevailing in Sicily. By the 2nd century the cult of Christianity had gained strength. This faith rejected traditional Roman gods and became a threat to the Roman emperors. Christians suffered frequent persecution for believing in their god's exclusivity and sometimes met with martyrdom. In Sicily the spread of Christianity encountered less hostility, and many Christians found a safer haven there. When Constantine legitimized Christianity in 313, it grew rapidly, and in 395 became the established religion of the Empire.

One of the early martyrs of the Christian church in Sicily was a young woman named Agatha, who was disfigured and tortured to death in 251 during the reign of Emperor Decius. According to legend, her breasts were cut off as punishment for spurning the advances of Quintanus, the governer of Sicily, and defying his command to abandon her faith. She became the patron saint of the city of Catania. Small, breast-shaped cakes called *minne di Sant'Agata* (St. Agatha's breasts) are dedicated to her. Elsewhere in Sicily the cakes are called *minne di vergini* (virgin's breasts).

The Vandals, Goths and Byzantines

Decadence and internal strife fueled the disintegration of the Roman Empire, opening the way for external forces to carve out pieces of the empire for themselves. Germanic peoples known as Vandals coming from what is now Scandinavia began migrating westward and southward. They became a formidable military force as their incursions into Roman territory met with success. After taking Carthage in North Africa from the Romans, they set their sights on Rome's Mediterranean island possessions. Sicily fell in 468 to the Vandals, who, in turn, relinquished Sicily in 493 to another invading Germanic people, the Goths. By 535, the Byzantines under the rule of Justinian ousted the Goths and annexed the island to the Greek-speaking Eastern Roman Empire, whose capital was Constantinople (formerly Byzantium). Sicily once again was immersed in Greek tradition. She became part of the Eastern Orthodox Church and continued to speak Greek, the language of her latest captors.

The Arabs

Sicily passed into the hands of Arab Muslims in 902 after a long, determined campaign. Arab raids on Byzantine Sicily began as early as the 7th century. The island of Pantelleria fell in 700. An invasion in 827 near Mazara del Vallo on the southwestern coast of Sicily was successful, and more cities were taken. But several subsequent sieges were necessary before they obtained complete control of the island in 902. Sicily became an emirate, with Palermo its capital, from which the Arabs ruled until 1091. Palermo became adorned with mosques and minarets alongside cathedrals. Under the Arabs' watch, Sicily became one of the wealthiest and most progressive cultures of medieval Europe.

The followers of Islam, also known as Saracens, began their assault on Sicily from modern-day Tunisia in North Africa. The group was comprised of Arabs originally from the Arabian peninsula, Spanish Muslims and the indigenous Berbers of North Africa, converts to the Muslim faith. They were destined to have a profound influence on Sicily and her cuisine.

The Arabs introduced advanced irrigation technology and revolutionized existing agricultural practices. They constructed canals to bring water from springs and rivers to agricultural areas and cities. In the cities, a network of underground tunnels (*kanat*) was dug, with the tunnels sloped downward for gravity-based water flow. This water system also fed city gardens and fountains. Remnants of these ancient tunnels still exist in some of the old parts of Palermo.

Arabs added a wide variety of new crops and were able to cultivate them on a large scale because of the improvements they had made in water availability. They broke up many of the vast feudal estates, the *latifundia,* into smaller farms and gardens, freeing the farmers who worked the plots from indentured servitude. Orchards of lemons, oranges, almonds, pistachios and mulberries were established. Sugar cane was grown in the flat coastal areas.

Date palms and carob trees were planted. Rice was introduced and was grown in paddies in the eastern part of the island near Lentini. Other new vegetables, fruits and spices brought by the Arabs included eggplant, artichoke, melon, apricot, banana, buckwheat, cumin, tarragon, jasmine and a white grape variety called *zibibbo*, which later would be used to make sweet wines.

Some scholars theorize that Arabs also introduced to Sicily the "naked" wheat variety known as durum wheat, asserting that it had not been grown, at least to any great extent, during Greek and Roman times when Sicily's extensive output of wheat was of a different "naked" variety known as soft bread wheat. We can leave this matter of debate to molecular archaeologists, because the salient point is that the Arabs introduced some foods of great significance that were made from the hard-grained durum wheat. The most far-reaching of them was dried pasta (*pasta secca*). Due to its high gluten content, dough made from durum wheat is strong. It can be rolled and cut into many forms that maintain their shapes and patterns, and lasting ridges can be impressed on the surface. When dried, the pasta does not spoil, thus making it suitable for long-term storage and transport. It had been known to the Arabs since about the 8th century. The Arabic word *itriyya* referred to long, thin strings of dough that were dried before boiling.

Itriyya had a tremendous influence on the island's foodways and far beyond. We know that by the 12th century dried pasta products were manufactured in Sicily for export. Al-Sharif al-Idrisi, an esteemed cartographer in the employ of Roger II, King of the Normans—whose father conquered Sicily and ended Arab rule—was commissioned to create an elaborate map of the world as it was then known. It was to be accompanied by a book detailing, among other things, commerce and production in all the locations shown on the map and visited by al-Idrisi in the 15 years he spent on the project. The map and book, interestingly entitled, *A Diversion for the Man Longing to Travel to Far-off Places*, were completed in 1154. The book records the presence of mills in the town of Trabia on the northern coast, near Palermo, which were making commercial preparations of dried pasta and shipping large quantities of it to the rest of Europe.

Arabs brought the art of making couscous, a painstaking process the Sicilians call *incocciata*, which involves rolling fine grains of durum wheat (semolina) in circles in a flat bowl while moistening it with water to form small, uniform granules. The granules are cooked by steaming over broth. In North Africa, couscous usually is topped with a meat stew. But in Sicily,

Involtini, rolls of thinly sliced meat wrapped around a filling. The rolls are skewered and grilled.

where fish are bountiful, couscous typically is topped with fish. In western Sicily, where the Arabic influence was particularly strong—especially in the city of Trapani—this dish (*cuscus alla Trapanese* or *cuscus di pesce*) continues to be popular. A recipe for *cuscus di pesce* is on p. 50.

Skewered and stuffed foods were also a part of the Arab legacy. Typical stuffing combinations include dried currants with bread crumbs. The embodiment of this kind of preparation is *involtini alla Siciliana,* Sicilian skewered meat rolls. Thin slices of veal or beef are rolled around a mixture of toasted bread crumbs, pine nuts, dried currants and cheese. Three or four of these rolls, interspersed with slices of onion and bay leaves, are placed on a skewer and grilled. A recipe for *involtini alla Siciliana* is on p. 59.

The Sicilian sweet tooth was diversified by the Arab's gift of sugar cane. Prior to this time, honey and a syrupy reduction of grape juice (*vino cotto*) were used as sweeteners. Each has a distinct flavor that tends to dominate in dishes. The use of cane sugar allowed for the creation of sweets with subtler flavors contributed by other ingredients. *Cannoli* ("pipes"), arguably Sicily's most famous dessert innovation with Arab roots, are crispy, fried, hollow tubes made of dough flavored with cinnamon. The addition of wine to the dough creates little air pockets that form and break during frying, giving the shells their characteristic pock-marked surface. The tubes are filled with sweetened ricotta cream, and the ends are decorated with some candied fruit. (For a recipe to make *cannoli,* see p. 67.) *Cassata,* the queen of Sicilian cakes, is assembled from layers of sponge cake and sweetened ricotta cheese surrounded by a shell of marzipan tinted pale green. The cake is iced and lavishly decorated with candied fruit and zucchini preserves. Marzipan itself has an Arab heritage and is used in many confections besides *cassata.* Most notable are the molded, vividly colored marzipan fruits.

Sugary frozen fruit treats were another Arab contribution. A *sorbetto* (from the Arabic *sciarbat*), or sorbet, is a frozen, water-based dessert, typically made with fruit juice and puréed fruit (see p. 70 for a recipe to make mandarin orange sorbet). In early times a *sorbetto* was concocted from the juice of citrus fruits and snow brought from the slopes of Mt. Etna. A variation is the *granita,* a refreshing drink of flavored, crushed ice.

Realistic peach-shaped confection made of sweetened almond paste (*marzipane*).

The Arabs left their imprint on the ritual of bluefin tuna fishing, an important industry in the Mediterranean since prehistory. Ensnaring tuna in some form of complex, giant undersea trap (*tonnara*) comprised of interconnected chambers made of net may have originated as early as Phoenician times. Arabs contributed some of the terminology of the *tonnara* as well as the music of the traditional songs and chants the men sang as they worked. Annually, in anticipation of the spawning migrations, the Arabs assembled a seven-chambered trap west of Sicily in the waters off Favignana, the southernmost of the Egadi Islands. The *rais* (Arabic for "head") led his crew of fishermen in carrying out the *mattanza* (Spanish for "killing"). First he determined that the migrating fish were successfully herded through the chambers via inter-chamber gates to the seventh and final chamber, the "Chamber of Death." This chamber had a net floor, which then was slowly raised, bringing the fish to the surface. Crowded together without possible escape and wildly thrashing, the fish were dispatched with barbed gaffs and hauled away. Today, overfishing has all but ended the capture of bluefin tuna in the Mediterranean.

The Norman French

Sicily came under the control of the Normans in 1091, after a protracted war that lasted 30 years. Originally from Scandinavia, the Normans settled in northern France in a region eventually named for them, Normandy, and they became Christians. Many left France to continue their pursuit of property and fortune, especially landless younger sons such as Roger Hauteville, youngest of twelve sons of a twice-wed nobleman. Hauteville and several of his brothers joined other Normans as mercenaries. Owing to their successful efforts on behalf of Pope Leo IX to wrest control of southern Italy from the remaining Byzantines, the ambitious Roger and his brother Robert were emboldened to launch a lengthy, but eventually victorious, assault to bring the infidels in Sicily under Norman control.

Palermo fell in 1072, following a string of early Norman successes in other Muslim strongholds on the island. Under the Normans, the city continued to be the capital of Sicily. Roger was made a count and established his administration in Palermo, retaining some Muslim civil servants whose knowledge proved invaluable in accomplishing a smooth transition to his rule. Count Roger's brother, Robert, became a duke and ruled over Apulia (Puglia) and Calabria in southern Italy, earlier Hauteville conquests. In less than twenty years, the remaining Muslim-controlled pockets in Sicily were overtaken.

Count Roger was an able statesman, and his reign was noted for restraint and religious tolerance. Mosques and synagogues were allowed to remain on the island. Muslims could worship as before and were free to maintain their own cultural traditions. Jews, thought to have settled in Sicily in the first century, lived almost exclusively within Jewish communities in the towns. They also were treated with some degree of tolerance, and their trade and artistic pursuits were encouraged. Arabic remained one of the official languages, along with Latin, Norman French and Greek. The agricultural landscape remained largely unchanged, as Muslim communities still existed to tend labor-intensive crops such as sugar cane and rice.

Count Roger was succeeded by his 16-year-old son, Roger II, who became the most esteemed of the Norman rulers. To unify and further strengthen his domain, which now included the regions in southern Italy formerly held by his uncle, Duke Robert, Count Roger II raised the status of his domain to a kingdom with papal blessing. In 1130 he and his heirs were granted the Crown of the Kingdom of Sicily, Calabria and Apulia. It became one of the wealthiest principalities in Europe.

Norman Sicily under King Roger II experienced a heightened interest in the Arabic way of life. Indeed, the King himself held court as if he were a caliph, even enjoying the requisite perk of a private harem. Distrusting his barons, King Roger chose Arabs to be his close advisers and attendants, and, not surprisingly, royal cooks. Thus Arab culinary tradition was kept alive in Sicily during Norman times. Normans themselves added little to the Sicilian menu besides dried cod (*stoccafisso*).

11

Bluefin tuna, up to 14 feet long, have been snared for centuries in elaborate net traps.

Religious intolerance gained a foothold under the successors of King Roger II. His son William I and grandson William II were ineffective at preventing attacks on Arabs by their bigoted, power-grabbing barons. Many Arabs left Sicily; others fled to temporary safety in the mountains or moved to the western end of the island. Urged by the Pope, Christian settlers from the Italian peninsula took over Arab villages. Many agricultural regions were deserted, and the sugar cane crop almost disappeared without adequate specialized labor. Fortunately, the Arab confectionery arts were not lost. Recipes were safely stowed in the convents and monasteries, where nuns continued to make the treats and give them as presents; much later, in harder times, they would sell the sweets to support their orders. Some recipes were eventually lost forever with the last nun to know them.

The Hauteville dynasty came to an end in 1194.

Other Europeans

Possession of Sicily changed often in subsequent centuries as rival European dynasties played out their disputes on the island. Sicily became a pawn and a provincial prize. There were a few fundamental additions to the cuisine during this time, but the main outside influences had already been absorbed.

Hohenstaufen

In 1198 Frederick II von Hohenstaufen ascended the throne, and the Crown of Sicily was held by the Germanic Hohenstaufen Dynasty. Frederick II was the son of the last direct descendent and heir of Roger I on the female side. His mother, Constance, a daughter of Roger II, had married Henry VI of the

Swabian house of Hohenstaufen, who was King of Germany and Emperor of the Holy Roman Empire.

The new King of Sicily was a protector of the Arabs remaining on the island, employing them in his personal retinue and armies. He soon advocated, however, that they give up their religion and assimilate their communities into the rest of Sicilian society. Rebellious Arabs disregarding his proclamation were summarily taken and shipped to Lucera, a military colony in Apulia on the Italian mainland. The only Arabs remaining on the island were converts to the Roman Catholic Church, who became part of what was by then a more homogenous population.

Agriculture, especially wheat cultivation, was a strong interest of Frederick II. He was attentive to the productivity of the land held by the Crown. He grew and exported his own wheat and allowed peasants the use of uncultivated land with the stipulation that they grow wheat on it.

Frederick II was a brilliant, enlightened monarch with an unlimited thirst for knowledge. He became known as *Stupor mundi et immutator mirabilis,* ("Wonder of the world and marvellous innovator") and ruled for over 50 years. His heirs were less able rulers, and the throne was lost in 1266 to the French Angevin Dynasty ruling from Naples. Sicilian independence was lost.

French Angevin

Charles, Duke of Anjou, was crowned King of Sicily and King of Naples, and he ruled from Naples. The occupation of Sicily by the French Angevin was brief. An incident known as the Sicilian Vespers put an end to the unpopular Angevin domination in 1282. Already rebellious over the excessive taxes levied on them by King Charles, the Sicilians were at a breaking point when an altercation occurred between French troops and Sicilians during Easter Monday celebrations in Palermo. Troops ordered to search Sicilian men for concealed weapons reportedly also searched women, fondling them indecently. A bloody uprising ensued and the Angevins ultimately were expelled from the island. The French were not in Sicily long enough for their culinary influences to be felt at this time.

Royal House of Aragon

Peter III of Aragon (today a part of northeastern Spain) gained control of the Kingdom of Sicily in 1282. The Kingdom of Naples was retained by the

French, effectively severing what had been known as the Kingdom of Two Sicilies and refueling bitter rivalries between them. The Aragonese ruled until 1492. During the reign of the Aragonese, the two Kingdoms would be reunited and split once more. Sicily's wheat remained central to any plan to annex the island. Wheat would feed an invader's kingdom and pay royal debts. Frequent warfare on Sicilian soil during this time, however, cruelly laid waste to much of the land. Enemies burned crops, orchards and forests in an attempt to eradicate agriculture and commerce, and starve the population into submission. The fishing industry, especially the bluefin tuna enterprises, suffered. In 1347 the Black Death (bubonic plague) brought its own devastation to Sicily, taking its toll on the population and further straining the workforce responsible for the island's productivity. Natural calamities—drought and pestilence—brought periodic times of famine. Yet despite all of this, the ravaged land was retilled and again produced high yields as before.

The Spanish

The Royal Houses of Aragon and Castile merged in 1469 with the marriage of Ferdinand of Aragon to Isabella of Castile. Sicily was part of the package.

The Spanish Inquisition pervaded Sicily just before the end of the 15th century. This was Ferdinand and Isabella's permanent solution to rid Spain and its possessions of religious minorities. Sicilian Jews were expelled in 1492, depleting the island of many artisans, doctors and traders—and capital. When the Arabs were evicted a few centuries earlier, Jews had replaced them to some extent in the agricultural sector, running the labor-intensive sugar-cane plantations and refineries. With the loss of the Jews the sugar industry suffered another setback, and by the end of the 1700s sugar had to be imported. Evicted Jews spread the legacy of Sicilian cuisine in the Italian peninsula and beyond.

Spain's maritime interests expanded at the end of the 15th century. One of the most far-reaching voyages was undertaken by Christopher Columbus, who discovered the New World instead of the route to the fabled Spice Islands. The impact of this voyage, called the Columbian Exchange, was profound. Both cultural and biological elements were exchanged between the New World and the Old World. Among the new foods Columbus brought back to Europe were the chile pepper, bell pepper, potato, bean, squash, corn, tomato, prickly pear and chocolate. Of these, potatoes and corn had less significance for Sicilians. Europeans were slow to accept the tomato. It belongs to the same family as the poisonous mandrake and nightshades, and was suspected to be poisonous as well. The Italians were the first Europeans to cook with the tomato, but their experimentation didn't begin for about a century after its introduction. Once accepted, the tomato became a quintessential ingredient in the Italian kitchen.

As few kings ever took up residence in Sicily, the island was run by a succession of viceroys. The Sicilian aristocracy became bloated, in part by an influx of newly created Spanish nobility. In the early 16th century a grand baronial cuisine (*cucina baronale*) evolved. Impoverished peasants created poor imitations of many fancy dishes of the patricians.

The extravagant dishes of the aristocracy often contained the new ingredient chocolate in savory preparations. An example is a rendition of *caponata,* the sweet-and-sour eggplant dish, that included octopus, toasted almonds and bitter cocoa. (For variations on *caponata* recipes see pp. 61 and 63.) This cuisine also paired meat with chocolate. One such treat from Modica is delicious little pastries resembling empanadas called *impanatigghi,* which are filled with a mixture of minced meat, chocolate, cinnamon, almonds, nutmeg, egg and sugar. The meat, however, is not detectable. *Impanatigghi* are topped with a sprinkling of powdered sugar and a daub of chocolate. Today in the town of Modica in southeastern Sicily, chocolatiers still prepare minimally adulterated, fine artisanal dark chocolate according to Aztec tradition, as had been done for the wealthy aristocrats who once populated the town.

Spain's domination of Sicily ended in 1713. Subsequently the island was briefly ruled from 1713 to 1720 by the House of Savoy from Piedmont and from 1720 to 1734 by Austrians.

Royal House of Bourbon

Members of the Bourbon Dynasty first reigned in France in the 1500s, but by the 1700s other principalities were headed by branches of the far-reaching Bourbon family. For the major part of the period between 1734 and 1860, Sicily and most of southern Italy (The Kingdom of Two Sicilies) had a king from the Spanish branch of the Bourbon Dynasty on the throne.

Impanatigghe, a little pastry filled with a mixture of minced meat and chocolate.

15

A brief interlude in the reign of the Bourbons, and one with significant culinary consequences, occurred with Napoleon's occupation of Naples in 1798. Bourbon King Ferdinand IV was stripped of his crown and replaced by Napoleon's brother. Lord Nelson brought the ousted Bourbon ruler and his court from Naples to safety in Palermo on his flagship. It was the first time Ferdinand IV had been to Sicily as King for over 40 years. The nobles brought with them their penchant for French *haute cuisine*. Often Sicily had been relegated to a backwater possession mainly valuable as a granary, and therefore the Sicilian aristocrats had been far from being the first to know the current trends in fashion, art and taste. After the Bourbon court arrived in Palermo, many Sicilian aristocrats acquired a prized status symbol, a French or French-trained chef called a *monzù* (after the French word *monsieur*), and feasted on lavish French dishes. Butter was introduced, as were the creamy and buttery sauces typical of French cooking. A few of the fancy preparations attributable to the culinary artistry of a *monzù* were the *timballi,* rich, baked dishes of pasta pressed in round molds, sometimes encased with pastry, and terrines containing succulent goose-liver pâtés.

Italian Unification

Sicily was spared a takeover by Napoleon and in the early 1800s became a British protectorate for about a decade. The Bourbons sought a British alliance to help them recover Naples, while the British viewed the alliance as a strategic relationship to prevent Napoleon from closing the Mediterranean trade routes. The British adopted a constitution for Sicily that would guarantee independence and institute long-overdue reforms. But all was for naught when Napoleon was finally defeated and Ferdinand IV was reinstalled in Naples.

With hopes for a constitution dashed, the Sicilians resorted to rebellion. Several unsuccessful insurrections preceded Giuseppe Garibaldi's attempt in 1860 to defeat the Bourbons and unify Italy on behalf of the Piedmont House of Savoy. The insurrection was a triumph. Within a couple of months of landing in Sicily, Garibaldi liberated all parts of the island except Messina. It would be free within a year. Victor Emmanuel, King of Piedmont, became the first king of a united Italy.

Independence, however, didn't bring autonomy or prosperity to Sicily—yet. Results of an 1860 plebiscite in Sicily showed that the island was almost 100% behind a unified Italian nation. But this remarkably high percentage belied the fact that there had been much ambiguity on the issues on the ballot and many Sicilians were illiterate. The central government reneged on its intention to allow regional self-government for Sicily, and the island benefited little from unification. Overwhelming poverty and chaos drove over a million Sicilians to the Americas and Australia in search of work, beginning in the late 1890s. Cash sent by these emigrants to relatives still living on the island gave Sicily's economy a desperately needed boost.

Economic hardship continued well into the 20th century. Sicily suffered loss of life and property during World War II. Palermo's shoreline still bears the scars of the conflict. In 1946 Sicily finally achieved regional autonomy from the rest of Italy. The situation slowly began to improve, and Sicily became a significant part of Italy's economy, with new industries, jobs and infrastructure. For centuries Sicily had very rudimentary roads. Those built by the Romans had fallen into disrepair long ago and transportation was largely limited to dirt tracks. In the 1800s the dirt roads were improved to allow wheeled traffic, and wooden carts drawn by mules supplanted walking or riding a mule as means of transportation for peasants. These ornately carved and colorfully painted carts were replaced in the 1960s by three-wheeled vehicles (*motorapi*). After World War II, economic improvements led to creation of long-needed superhighways that now connect much of the island.

Agriculture expanded considerably; an impressive variety of crops are now cultivated commercially. Large areas are devoted to growing artichokes, cardoons, olives, eggplant, melons, prickly pear, tomatoes, potatoes, citrus fruits and grapes. Sicily also has become a successful producer of fine wines. Fortunately, the cuisine of Sicily remains firmly tied to its roots. Families typically cook traditional dishes, eschewing fast food options, and the majority of restaurants offer classic fare so tourists can experience the traditional tastes of Sicily.

Throughout much of Sicilian history, celebration of the many religious holidays during each year has been associated with special foods. This also is a lasting tradition, and one could easily plan a trip to catch a particular festival. A good place to start would be the feast day of St. Joseph (San Giuseppe) on March 19th. Magnificent altars to St. Joseph are constructed of bread in gratitude for fulfillment of promises made and favors granted, deliverance from famine, and for blessings for a successful new harvest. The altars are built of elaborately constructed breads, all objects of art. The bread often is arranged in a tableau, with each bread constructed to fit in its correct place in the design. Where else but in Sicily would wheat reach such a level of art!

Provinces of Sicily

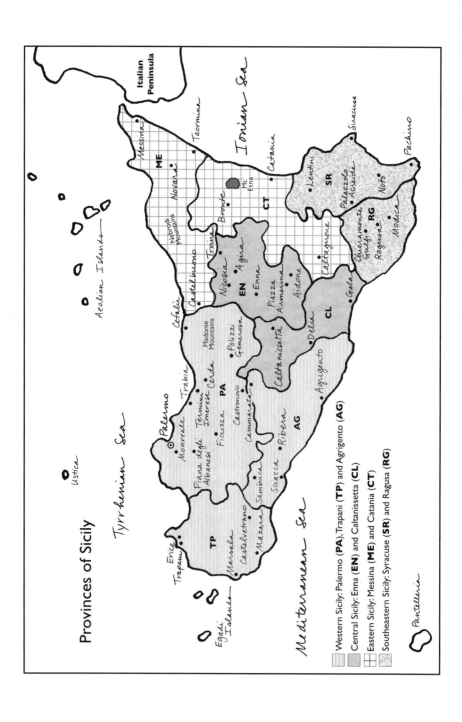

Western Sicily: Palermo (**PA**), Trapani (**TP**) and Agrigento (**AG**)

Central Sicily: Enna (**EN**) and Caltanissetta (**CL**)

Eastern Sicily: Messina (**ME**) and Catania (**CT**)

Southeastern Sicily: Syracuse (**SR**) and Ragusa (**RG**)

Local Sicilian Food

A Quick Tour of Sicilian Foods and Their Local Variations

Sicilian Food in a Nutshell

Food is of paramount importance in Sicily—so much so that people tend (or would like) not to abandon their eating habits for health reasons. Even in these rapidly changing times many families still gather for the midday meal, which tends to be quite a long affair, especially on Sundays.

Sicilian food shares with the cooking of the rest of the Mediterranean region the tradition of a strong emphasis on (mostly white) wheat products accompanied by a variety of vegetables (the famous Mediterranean diet). In the old days a typical peasant lunch was simply bread and onions (*pane e cipolle*), maybe with a little cheese.

Bread (*pane*) was and still is considered essential to fill one's belly and to accompany any food except the first course of a meal, which typically is pasta or (more rarely) rice. Most Sicilians, especially those over the age of 50, find it impossible to eat an antipasto or a vegetable dish without fresh bread. The importance, even sacredness, of bread resulted in the creation of the incredible variety of shapes and kinds of bread still available throughout the island. It is baked in most Sicilian bakeries twice a day, because Sicilians love fresh bread so much that they take the time to buy it twice a day. Bread that is only hours old may be considered practically inedible, so many traditional Sicilian recipes make use of bread crumbs (*pangrattato; mollica* in Sicilian) as a way to recycle stale bread. They often are stir-fried (*atturrata*) in a pan with a little oil, chopped onions, grated cheese, pine nuts and currants. This mixture is used as the filling in *involtini,* stuffed rolls of meat, fish or eggplant, which are among the most typical Sicilian recipes (see *Recipes,* pp. 57, 59). Today most people buy bread crumbs rather than grating them.

Most Sicilians eat spaghetti (or other kinds of pasta) every day; even dogs are fed pasta daily in Italy. Pasta can be tossed with virtually any kind of dressing: simple olive oil, garlic and red pepper (as in *pasta aglio olio peperoncino,* also called *alla carrettiera*); or cheese, meat, vegetables or fish; or a combination of ingredients (as in *pasta con salsiccia e ricotta,* pasta with sausage and ricotta cheese, or *pasta con pescespada e zucchini,* pasta with swordfish and zucchini). Besides old favorites such as *pasta con melanzane* or *alla Norma* (pasta with eggplants, tomato sauce and grated, salted ricotta cheese), a plethora of new recipes have already become classic. Pistachio pesto (*pesto di pistacchio*) is a good example. It is featured in a recipe for *pennette con pesto di pistacchio e mandorle* on p. 45. Tomato sauce is an important ingredient, but it never accompanies pasta in the quantity Americans typically put on their plates.

Rice (*riso*) is not grown in Sicily today, as it would require too much water. Climatic changes in the 1800s left the island too arid. There is only one important Sicilian rice dish: *arancine* ("little oranges"), deep-fried rice balls, so named because of their round shape and golden color. Crunchy on the outside, the rice balls have a surprise on the inside—tasty fillings of cheese, ham or other meat. Pizza, said to have been invented in Naples, is very popular all over Italy (and the world!). Sicily is no exception to this rule; there are many kinds of typically Sicilian pizza. The classic example is *sfincione,* a thick pizza topped with tomato sauce, onions, *caciocavallo* cheese, toasted bread crumbs and oregano.

The lack of meat proteins prevalent in the past was compensated by a variety of soups of legumes (*zuppe* or *minestre di legumi*), such as beans (*fagioli*), chickpeas (*ceci*), fava beans (*fave*) and lentils (*lenticchie*), in which broken spaghetti pieces (*spaghetti tagliati*) or small kinds of pasta were cooked. Such soups are still popular winter foods in Sicily. Dry beans are normally used (in which case they need at least a few hours of soaking before cooking), but fresh brown beans are available in summer and are enjoyed in summer soups.

Sicilian cuisine is highly inventive with vegetables (*verdure*), whose quality and

Sicilian bread is made in many intriguing shapes, including this serpentine *scaletta.*

freshness are normally very good. Depending on the type of vegetable, they can be pickled, stuffed (usually without ground beef), boiled and then salted in the pan with olive oil and garlic, deep-fried with or without batter, stewed, grilled, or served raw in salads, which are almost invariably dressed with salt, olive oil (*olio d'oliva*) and vinegar (*aceto*) or fresh lemon juice (*succo di limone*). Some vegetable dishes, most famously eggplant *caponata,* are sweet-and-sour. The availability of vegetables changes throughout the year. Among the most common vegetables, cauliflower, broccoli, fennel and squash are winter crops, while artichokes, fresh peas and fresh fava beans are available in the spring, and tomatoes, eggplants and sweet peppers are associated with summer. Seasonal availability tends to be less important today because of greenhouses, which are especially dense in the southeastern provinces of Sicily.

Some vegetables, such as *zucchina lunga,* are unique to Sicily. This light green zucchini, about two feet long, surprises visitors to Sicily, including mainland Italians. It is usually cut and fried, and its leaves (*tenerumi*) are also eaten. The yellow blossoms of regular zucchini (*fiori di zucca*) are a delicacy. Many vegetables are pickled; pickled eggplant (*melanzane sottaceto*) is especially popular. Some are sun-dried, especially tomatoes cut into halves (*pomodori secchi*). Sun-dried purée of fresh tomatoes, or tomato extract (*estratto di pomodoro*), is a uniquely Sicilian product, not to be confused with commercial tomato paste. *Estratto di pomodoro* is used in many traditional Sicilian recipes.

Sicilians forage for and eat a very wide variety of wild vegetables (*verdure amare*), which are given different names in different parts of the island. Sicily was very poor until the 1960s, and foraging for wild vegetables was essential for survival. *Verdure amare* are usually bitter and need to be boiled in copious amounts of water to become palatable. The older generations have a special liking for them, even though most can now afford to buy other foods. Urban dwellers or those who have no time to forage for themselves can purchase these vegetables from itinerant vendors who sell them from their small trucks in the main cities and towns. Land snails (*lumache*), several kinds of which live on the island, are also often collected by Sicilians in the countryside. These traditions of foraging for wild vegetables and land snails are losing favor among the younger generations and may soon be lost.

Garlic, onions, parsley, mint, rosemary, oregano and bay leaves are among the most common flavors used in Sicilian cuisine. Many herbs grow wild in fields and woods, Sicilian oregano being especially famous for its fragrance. All over Italy a powdered coloring agent is used to impart a saffron color to

Artichoke (*carciofo; cacocciulo* in Sicilian), a popular vegetable making its appearance early in spring. Sicilian artichokes are small, tender and sometimes purple.

risotto. In Sicily this powder is also used to color pasta in dishes such as pasta with stir-fried cauliflower (*pasta con i broccoli arriminati*). Potatoes also may be colored yellow with this powder or with true saffron as in *bollito con patate e zafferano* (see *Recipes,* p. 58). Sicilian cuisine tends to make extensive use of certain combinations of ingredients; this is especially true for pine nuts and currants, and for green olives and capers, which are often used together.

Olives deserve special attention, as they are the source of the only truly Sicilian cooking oil: olive oil (*olio di oliva*). Traditional Sicilian dishes do not call for butter; small quantities of lard are used to make sweets associated with festivities such as Christmas or Carnival. Although most olives are pressed, a small percentage of the total crop is cured to be sold as table olives, either black (*olive nere*) or green (*olive bianche,* literally, "white olives"). Both kinds come from the same tree, the difference being if they are picked from the tree when ripe (black) or unripe (green). There is a whole culture of olives; subtle distinctions in their quality and curing determine at least a dozen types with different names and prices. Among black olives, some of the most appreciated are the ones with very wrinkled and opaque skin. These have been left to fully ripen on the tree or are picked from the ground, and they are called *olive al fiore* (*olive acciurate* in Sicilian), "blossoming olives," even though the tree has no flowers at this stage.

Until recently, the great majority of Sicilians ate very little meat. In the countryside they could only afford to eat meat once or twice a year, when animals were butchered for special festivities. Pigs (*maiali*) were butchered mainly for Carnival, a time for revelling and eating big meals before the forty long days of fasting for Lent. In honor of Jesus Christ's resurrection, Easter was (and still is) the time to kill lambs (*agnelli*) and kids (*capretti*). They are expensive and still usually constitute the main course of Easter Sunday dinner. In the countryside, the cheaper meat of castrated sheep (*castrato;* male sheep are castrated to make their meat more tender and more similar to lamb) is often grilled or barbecued for family holiday gatherings. Easter Monday and the national holidays of April 25th and May 1st are the traditional days for family outings, somewhat like Labor Day in the United States.

In poor countries all parts of the animals are eaten. Sicily was no exception to that rule in its poorer days, and tripe (boiled and sliced), liver, brain and kidneys are still sold in Sicilian butcher shops. Today most Sicilians eat meat almost daily. Beef is called *manzo;* veal is *vitello.* Sicilian veal is not white meat, and comes from a larger animal than American veal. Beef is seldom served as a thick, juicy steak. Meat tends to be cut thin, and it is pounded even thinner for use in recipes such as stuffed meat rolls, which can be small (*involtini*) and cooked on skewers or rather large (*braciolone* and *falsomagro*) and served sliced. Because meat has been scarce for most of Sicily's history, there are few other inventive Sicilian meat recipes.

Horse meat has a long tradition in major Sicilian cities. It is sold in separate butcher shops and counts some real aficionados, who believe it is tastier and more nutritious than other kinds of meat. Mules and donkeys used to be ubiquitous in the countryside, where they were employed for transportation, and where donkey milk was highly recommended for children. Donkeys, especially, are very rare today—a striking difference from the past.

Turkey, guinea fowl, goose, duck and rabbit are present on the island, but not very common. Centuries of intense hunting have taken their toll on game in Sicily. The few remaining forests have been repopulated with wild boars, whose numbers are increasing. Outside of nature reserves, they can be legally hunted, but a good number are also bred on farms. Black pigs are another novelty. Previously present only in the Nebrodi Mountains, black pigs now are bred in different areas and served in several restaurants on the island. Boars, black pigs, and regular pork are used to make sausage and salami, which usually are of excellent quality in the smaller towns where they are locally produced.

Chicken is commonly eaten—specialized shops sell grilled chicken (*pollo arrosto*) to take out—but there are few interesting chicken recipes in Sicilian cuisine. Sicilians do eat chicken at home, but don't feel it is remarkable enough for a restaurant outing. Because chicken is popular with many tourists, chicken dishes do sometimes appear on menus in restaurants that cater to tourists (see *Recipes,* p. 55). In the past many people in the country or in the outskirts of cities kept chickens near their home, and left them free to roam around. For these people eggs were a natural source of protein. Eggs are still an important part of the Sicilian diet, although today people typically buy commercially farmed eggs at the grocery store. Virtually any variation on the omelet (*frittata*) theme is possible; *frittate* can be made with ricotta cheese and spinach, with shrimp (*gamberi*), green beans (*fagiolini*) or any other kind of vegetable. Omelets with wild vegetables such as wild asparagus (*asparago selvatico*) are especially popular.

Fish used to be abundant near the Sicilian coast, but the poor condition of the roads meant that fish was not readily available in the interior. This lack of seafood in the diet often resulted in iodine deficiency and goiter among people in the interior villages of Sicily and Pantelleria. What fish did arrive came on Friday, the traditional day for eating fish, because the Catholic Church proscribed the eating of meat on Friday. The tradition of eating fish on Friday persists, though the Church ban does not.

Fish has become more and more rare in the sea and very expensive. Still, Sicilians have a special liking for fish, even those with a strong "fishy" flavor. In general, fish is in great demand and its flavor and smell are considered to be something to enhance, not to hide with heavy sauces. Sicilians are fully aware of the importance of freshness to the delicious flavor of fish. Italian law now requires labels indicating the provenance and date of catch of fresh seafood. But itinerant fishmongers and those with small shops do not always follow the law!

Many kinds of fish (*pesce*) are unique to the Mediterranean and may be unfamiliar to visitors. As in the rest of Italy, in Sicily it usually is served with bones, head, and tail. Americans may find this presentation difficult to handle. On the other hand, deboning fish is a certain way to deprive it of its flavor. Fish is commonly grilled very simply and dressed with *ammogghiu,* a Sicilian term for a mixture of olive oil, garlic and parsley, with fresh lemon juice, which is likely to be served with the fish on the table. (The dressing is called *salmoriglio* in Italian.) Many kinds of seafood (called sea fruits, *frutti di mare,* in Italian) are available, but some are scarcer than in the past and therefore very expensive. Fish and other seafood can be grilled, fried or stewed with garlic, olive oil and a few fresh tomatoes. Octopus (*polpo*), which is usually boiled, is a perennial favorite, dressed with olive oil and lemon juice; squid and cuttlefish (*seppie*) are either stuffed, grilled or stewed. Baby fish (*neonata*) are in high demand, but their fishing is now restricted by law. Sicilians make omelets with them. Sea urchins (*ricci*) are cut open and sold in the streets near the sea. Their eggs are considered delicious on their own and also are used to dress pasta. Another seafood product commonly used to dress pasta is cuttlefish ink (*nero di seppia*), which colors the pasta black. Some chefs are experimenting with new ways of using this product, such as in the recipe for pasta with cuttlefish and pistachios on a bed of cuttlefish ink (*cavati con seppie e pistacchi di bronte*) on p. 47.

Swordfish (*pesce spada*) and tuna (*tonno*) are cooked in different ways and are very important fish on the island. Moreover, both are served smoked (*affumicato*) or raw (*carpaccio*), and are a very popular antipasto in towns and cities all over the coasts of Sicily. Their importance in different parts of Sicily is discussed in our overview of her provinces. A wide variety of bluefish (*pesce azzurro*), including fresh sardines (*sarde*) and mackerel (*sgombri*), are eaten in Sicily. Bluefish tend to be smaller and have more bones than white fish. They also are much less expensive.

Sicily has a great tradition of quality cheeses, designated *DOP* to certify that the method of production is traditional to the location. The most common Sicilian cheeses are *caciocavallo* from cow's milk and pecorino from sheep's (*pecora*) milk. In earlier stages of ripeness these cheeses are less salty and less seasoned. These younger cheeses are *tuma* (unsalted), *primosale* (lightly salted) and *primintiu* (rather salted) cheeses. Many other kinds of cheeses are imported from their places of origin on mainland Italy. Parmesan (uniquely from Parma) and gorgonzola (from the town in Lombardy with the same name) are among them. Some other "foreign" cheeses are reproduced locally with decent results.

Ricotta means "re-cooked." It is a by-product of cheese-making, made by re-cooking the whey of cheese with additional milk. The best, tastiest, and fattiest ricotta is made from sheep's milk. Sheep's milk ricotta is so popular that there is not enough sheep's milk to satisfy the demand. Sicilians use ricotta

Caciocavallo, a mild cow's milk cheese that is stretched and shaped by hand into a pear shape with a knob on top.

25

extensively, either as is (for dressing pasta) or mixed with sugar to become creamy (*crema di ricotta*) for the manufacture of sweets, such as the world-famous *cannoli* and *cassata*. Ricotta is very perishable, maintaining its freshness no longer than 24–48 hours.

Sicilians love fruit and typically end their meals with it—it is the most common kind of dessert. Like vegetables, fruits tend to be served seasonally, despite the fact that greenhouses now make it possible to have (very expensive and not very tasty) fruit in any season. The Sicilian climate allows almost all kinds of fruit to be grown locally and to be available fresh and generally of very good quality.

Citrus groves dot the landscape, and Sicilian citrus fruits (*agrumi*) are among the best in the world. Sicilians often eat them with a pinch of salt. Oranges (*arance*) and tangerines (*manderini*) are winter crops, whereas lemons (*limoni*) are available all year round. Orange salad (*insalata di arance*) is a typically Sicilian side dish, though not often found in restaurants. Another typical citrus species is the citron (*cedro*), which is sometimes truly enormous. Citrons are not as sour as lemons, and they are often sold as a snack in markets and streets. Sicilians peel and cut them, then eat the fruit, including the thick pith. A pinch of salt is mandatory! Some citrus fruits, such as *lumie,* which are smaller and less sour than lemons, have virtually disappeared, and others, such as the lime (*limetta*), which is practically unknown to Sicilians, never arrived. Grapefruit (*pompelmo*) is a novelty that is slowly gaining ground. But most Sicilians still don't know what to do with it.

Medlars (*nespole*) are the first summer fruit to arrive, already ripening in May. Although introduced to Sicily fairly recently (in the 19th century), they are quite rooted in Sicilian culture. A masterpiece of Italian literature, the late 19th-century novel *I Malavoglia, "The House of the Medlar Tree,"* by Catanese novelist Giovanni Verga, gave the fruit literary recognition.

Almonds (*mandorle*) are grown extensively in Sicily, and they have proven to be among the best in the world. Almonds are used in many Sicilian sweets. In June they are sold fresh, before sun-drying. Their green shell at this stage is so soft that it can be cracked open with one's teeth. Fresh almonds are covered with a thin, yellow, inner skin, which must be removed. The time spent performing this task and discovering the delicious flavor of the white almond inside is a memorable summertime pleasure.

The fig tree grows almost by itself in Sicily, as it does not require much work, except picking the delicious fresh green figs (*fichi freschi*) in August. Rare black figs ripen in winter (*fichi d'inverno*). Dried figs (*fichi secchi*) are

Citron (*cedro*), a knobby, yellow citrus
fruit enjoyed for its pulp and pith.

used in the manufacture of some Sicilian
sweets.

Many other fruits are available in summer:
mulberries (*gelsi*) both white and black,
cherries (*ciliege*) and sour cherries (*amarene*),
used mostly used for jams and syrups. Cold
slices of watermelon (*anguria*) sold in the
streets are a refreshing snack. A few other
kinds of melons and cantaloupes are
available, but the choice is not large.

Chestnut trees grow in Sicilian mountains,
and in the fall when they ripen, chestnuts
(*castagne*) are grilled over charcoal and sold
warm in the streets. Another popular fall
product is the persimmon (*kaki* or *loti*).
Prickly pears, which are called *fichi d'india*,
"Indian figs," even though they originated in the Americas, are another
autumn treat sold in the streets by vendors who usually are ready to peel
them for customers to eat on the spot. They come in different colors, which
do not affect their taste. There are so many seeds in the pulp that is impossible
to spit them out or avoid them in any way. Sicilians learn at an early age to
munch the pulp and swallow without biting into the seeds, but this task
might be a challenge for a visitor. It is well worth a try, though, as prickly
pears are delicious—especially when the rains in late October and November
make the fruits softer and sweeter. There are plans to develop seedless prickly
pears (which purists oppose), but they have not appeared on the market yet.

Sicilian cuisine reaches its creative peak in the manufacturing of sweets
(*dolci*). An astonishing quantity and variety of sweets fill the pastry shops
(*pasticcerie*), and most Sicilians eat *dolci* on Sundays, holidays and any special
occasion. A *pasticceria* can be simply a shop where it is possible to buy sweets
to take home or to offer as a gift, and not necessarily a place to eat them. But
pasticcerie also can be accompanied by a coffee bar (simply *bar* in Italian),
where one can purchase beverages and other foods to eat on the go. As a rule,
every *pasticceria*, accompanied by a *bar* or not, has its own pastry chef
(*pasticcere*), and produces its own fresh *dolci* every day. The sign *produzione
propria*, which means that the goods are produced by the owners, is
important to most customers, who are fully aware of the importance of the
freshness and quality of sweets. Coffee bars often produce other sweets that

go well with espresso coffee for breakfast or midmorning snacks. *Cornetti* (croissants) with chocolate, custard or almond filling are very popular. The variety of sweets available for breakfast in coffee bars has steadily increased in recent decades.

By far the main purpose of Sicilian bakeries (*panifici*) is to make bread; in most cases bread represents 90%–95% of their production. In the last few decades *panifici* have diversified their offerings, producing other goods, called *prodotti da forno* (baked products), some of which are sweet, but very different from what Sicilian normally refer to as *dolci*. Among these are pies (*torte*) and especially dry biscuits (*biscotti*), a large variety of which traditionally exists in Sicily. Unlike other countries, where biscuits tend to be greasy with butter, Sicily's *biscotti* have honey (as in *nucatoli*) or almonds (as in *quaresimali*) or *vino cotto* ("cooked wine," as in certain types of *mostaccioli*) among their ingredients. *Prodotti da forno* can also be *salati*, "salted,"meaning savory, as opposed to sweet. These are mostly different kinds of pizzas, all rather thick, baked in the bakery's electric ovens and sold by weight—very different from the pizzas made in pizzerias, which are thin and baked in large, circular brick ovens fed with wood. Some *panifici* and most coffee bars also produce a large variety of other types of *rosticceria*, a large category of food encompassing pizzas, *calzoni, arancine,* and so on. *Rosticcerie* can also be separate shops.

Sicilian *dolci* are normally quite elaborate and very sweet, but even people who find them too sweet agree they are beautiful to look at. Some, especially the famous *cassata,* have truly baroque decorations. This cake, constructed of sponge cake pieces, marzipan and sweet ricotta cream, is elaborately decorated with icing, candies, and fruit preserves. Most people do not even attempt to achieve the same result at home and simply buy their *dolci* in a *pasticceria,* since only the *pasticcere* has the required professional training, specific tools and special ingredients, such as the *zuccata* (zucchini preserves) used to decorate the *cassata*, to make perfect *dolci*.

Sicilian *dolci* can very be roughly divided into categories. One group is filled with highly perishable sweet ricotta cheese (*crema di ricotta,* "ricotta cream," used for *cannoli* and *cassata,* for example), custard (*crema gialla*), or whipped cream (*panna*). Others fall into the large category of *dolci da riposto* ("sweets for the cupboard"), which may become a little drier, but can be stored for a long time, and are ideal to keep in reserve at home in case of unexpected visitors. These include cookies and biscuits made with ground almonds (*mandorle*), or filled with a mixture of dried figs, walnuts and almonds (*conserva*) or with citron preserves (*cedrata*). Another category of sweets are fried (such as *sfinci,* a sort of doughnut). There are hundreds of *dolci* typical of one city or one town, some of which are listed in the *Menu Guide* and described later in this chapter. Sicilian *dolci* are considered very tasty, even those that are quite sweet.

In the past, and even today, some kinds of sweets and biscuits are also homemade. This is especially true for *dolci* typical of Christmas and other holidays. Many *dolci* used to be manufactured by cloistered nuns, who were totally secluded from the outside world. Hundreds of nuns filled the convents of the past, but there are very few today. Making and selling *dolci* was a way for the nuns to keep busy, to make some money for the convent, and also to communicate with the world. To keep the nuns secluded, transactions occurred through a rotating wheel somewhat like a lazy susan. Customers put the money on the wheel, then turned it to send the money inside the convent. The nuns took the money and placed the *dolci* on the wheel. Another rotation delivered the goods, with no direct contact between the public and the nuns.

Ice creams (*gelati*) and ices (*granite*), defined by many as Sicilian passions, deserve special recognition, and they are now imitated in ice cream parlors all over the world. *Gelati* are much more than desserts; in Sicily they can be eaten any time, any place, and, in major cities, even any time of the year. Ice cream parlors (*gelaterie*) are usually on the same premises as coffee bars and *pasticcerie,* and produce their own "fresh" ice cream and *granite*, ices made with different kinds of fruit. Lemon, strawberry and black mulberry are the classic *granite* flavors, but recently virtually every other kind of fruit has been added to the list. In the summer the production and consumption of *gelati* can be truly enormous, especially in the most famous *gelaterie,* because it includes what people eat on the premises and also what they buy to take home or to offer as gifts. Most *gelaterie* have at least a dozen flavors available, and new kinds are invented all the time. *Gelati* are not real ice creams; fruit flavors have very little, if

Marzipan engagement heart (*cuoricini per i fidanzati*) created by the late Corrado Costanza in his *pasticceria* in Noto.

any, cream among the ingredients. For flavors like chocolate, hazelnut, pistachio, and *bacio* (from the name of very popular milk-chocolate candies), there may be some cream, but usually *crema rinforzata,* milk with cornstarch, is used. Except for one flavor (*zuppa inglese,* "English soup"), eggs are not used in traditional Sicilian *gelati.*

Naturally, *gelati* are eaten on cones (*coni*) or in cups (*coppetta*) of different sizes. But in a surprising practice unique to Sicily *gelati* are also eaten in brioches! *Gelati* are also manufactured into real cakes of round (*torta gelato*) or oblong (*tronchetto,* "trunk") shape. Small pieces of *gelati,* artistically shaped in miniature cones or cups, are sold by weight in various flavors to satisfy the tastes of different people.

Sicilians drink wine (*vino*) and mineral water (*acqua minerale*) during meals. *Acqua minerale* is always sold as an extra. It is served cold, but without ice (*ghiaccio*), which is less widely available than in the United States. Milk (*latte*) is confined to breakfast, and virtually nonexistent for many people who prefer to get their calcium from cheeses and other dairy products instead. Soft drinks such as Coca-Cola are popular with the younger generation, especially during outings, but still not often consumed with meals at home. Beer (*birra*) is gaining popularity, especially in the summer, to accompany pizza or other *rosticceria* products. Birra Messina is the only brand of Sicilian beer.

Grapes, wheat and the olive tree are often referred to as the sacred triad of the Mediterranean, since their products (wine, bread and olive oil, respectively) have been considered sacred foods since prehistoric times. Wine is the natural accompaniment to a Sicilian meal. Sicily makes both red and white wines. Most Sicilians refill their own container with unbottled wine (*vino sfuso*) for everyday consumption and buy bottled wine only for special occasions. *Vino sfuso* sold at a winery or tavern can be of very good quality—almost as good as bottled—at one-tenth the cost. The quality of *vino sfuso* sold in restaurants is often not very good.

Vino sfuso tends to be rather high in alcohol content (13%–14%). In spite of this, the incidence of alcohol problems used to be rather limited in Sicily. Only recently have the sale and consumption of wine been subject to legal restriction, and, for the most part, wine is still considered a drink like any other. Before the arrival of Coca-Cola, children used to be given wine diluted with water (even if they did not really like it). The quality and variety of wines produced on the island have greatly improved in recent years, and Sicilian wines are booming all over the world. A description of wines is beyond the scope of this book, but some important local wines will be mentioned as we discuss the provinces of Sicily.

Sicilians often end their dinner with sweet wine, *amaro* (bitter digestive liqueur) or *limoncello,* a lemon liqueur originally from Sorrento, which has become enormously popular all over Italy. Espresso coffee is never missing at the very end.

Sicilians love to eat in the open (and everywhere, for that matter). As a result, in the summer and whenever weather permits (and it often does), restaurants and cafés in Sicily have outdoor tables. Vendors sell nuts of various kinds (*scaccio*) and other inexpensive and usually very tasty snacks (*rosticceria*) to munch on the streets. Many fried foods sold in fry shops (*friggitorie*) also are taken to go and eaten on the run.

The Provinces of Sicily

Sicily, with an area of 25,706 sq km (9,926 sq mi), is the largest island in the Mediterranean Sea. Because of its many mountains, transportation of goods and people in Sicily was (and to some extent still is) difficult. It used to be much easier to travel by sea than by land; days and days were needed to travel in the interior, a painstaking and uncomfortable experience. The result is that, even though there is a Sicilian culture common to the entire island, there are different customs, traditions, language and foods in different cities and towns, to a degree that may be hard for Americans to imagine for an area about as large as the state of Vermont.

Sicily is the largest of Italy's twenty regions and, from an administrative viewpoint, it is divided into nine provinces, which may grouped in the following manner: western (Palermo, Trapani, Agrigento), central (Enna, Caltanissetta), eastern (Messina, Catania) and southeastern (Syracuse, Ragusa). The provincial boundaries are not to be taken rigidly from a cultural viewpoint, as many towns share the culture of two or more provinces. Physical barriers such as those created by the Madonie and the Nebrodi Mountain ranges tend to define culture more than political boundaries do.

The isolation of some of the smaller islands has led to the evolution of their distinctive qualities. Ustica, which lies north of Palermo; Pantelleria and Linosa, which lie southwest of Sicily; and the seven Aeolian Islands off the northeastern coast in the province of Messina are all volcanic, with Vulcano and Stromboli being among the few active volcanoes in Italy. The three Egadi

Islands off the westernmost tip in the province of Trapani are not volcanic, but have rugged and beautiful mountains, while Lampedusa, which is quite far to the southwest—actually closer to Africa than to Sicily—is flat and barren, but has clear waters and beautiful beaches.

There is quite a lot of difference between the coastal areas, where the cuisine naturally centers on fish and seafood, and the interior of the island, where meat and vegetables predominate.

Western Sicily (Palermo, Trapani and Agrigento)

Tuna once constituted one of the main protein sources in Sicily; along the coasts there were 108 tuna fisheries (*tonnare*), with a special concentration in the westernmost tip of the island. In the month of May the fisheries awaited the arrival of the once huge schools of spawning tuna. At the end of the 19th century, the multimillionaire Florio family purchased a prosperous tuna industry in Favignana, one of the Egadi Islands, where the most famous Sicilian tuna fishery is still active and tuna continue to be fished in the traditional manner using a complex series of nets. Even today fresh tuna (*tonno; tunnina* in Sicilian) is available in the markets only in the month of May. Trapani is known for its variety of tuna dishes, such as *polpette di tonno* (tuna balls). The province also makes preserved tuna products, such as *salame, lattume* (sperm in olive oil) and *mosciame* (salted tuna), which are rarely found on the rest of the island. On the other hand, *tonno affumicato* (smoked tuna) and *bottarga* (salted, pressed tuna roe), also manufactured mostly in Trapani, are gaining popularity and are readily available in larger Sicilian cities.

The provinces of Trapani and its Egadi Islands offer many seafood specialties, including the excellent *spaghetti in brodo di aragosta* (spaghetti in lobster broth). In the town of Marsala people are particularly fond of a fried fish locally called *piscirè* (*donzelle* in Italian). Couscous is the perfect example of the Arabic influence in Sicilian cuisine, which has adopted this North African creation as an accompaniment to fish and fish broth. In the province of Trapani, both in restaurants and in homes, the tradition of making couscous by hand is still alive. In this process (*incocciato*), the couscous is made in a terra cotta pot (*mafaradda),* covered with a blanket (*cutra*), and then steamed in a special pot (*cuscusiera*). In the old days, when all couscous was made by hand, the "rejects" from the *incocciatura* procedure—grains that came out too large, called *frascatole*—were not discarded, but cooked in fish broth.

Today, the larger-grained *frascatole* are made deliberately, and some Trapani restaurants have revived this "poor" relative of couscous.

In this part of the island, pizza is very often a *rianata*, made with plenty of oregano. *Pesto trapanese,* a local contribution to pasta dressings, usually accompanies *busiate,* a type of pasta that often is available fresh. In the past *busiate* were shaped by hand by wrapping the dough around knitting needles (*busi*). The black bread *pane nero,* made with a rare kind of wheat called *tumminia,* is a specialty of Castelvetrano that has earned special recognition from the Slow Food International Movement.

Cassatelle (fried turnovers filled with sweet ricotta cream) are a delicious specialty of Trapani. Marsala has a local version of *cassatelle,* called *cappidduzzi,* and a type of biscuit, *tagliancozzi,* perfect for dipping in the world-famous Marsala wine.

The picturesque town of Erice is famous for the almond sweets formerly made by its cloistered nuns. Erice's many convents are now empty, but Maria Grammatico, who was raised in one of them as a child, still makes the pastries for her shop there. Her recipe for Genovesi, small custard-filled cakes that are heavenly when eaten warm from the oven, is reproduced on p. 68.

The island of Pantelleria, which is also in the province of Trapani, has several local specialties, known and available only there, including *ravioli panteschi, ciakiciuka* and *baci panteschi.*

The variety and quality of Sicilian wines is increasing steadily. The province of Trapani is almost totally cultivated in vineyards, which produce several kinds of table wines, sweet dessert wines (including Marsala) and a famous bitter digestive liqueur (*amaro Averna*). Sambuca, in Agrigento, makes an anise-flavored liqueur that carries the same name, and Erice makes a mint-flavored liqueur (*ericino*). Pantelleria is famous for its *passito,* made from locally grown grapes (especially of the rare and very sweet *zibibbo* variety) that have been left in special vats to become super-ripe (hence the name *passito,* which means "withered").

The city of Palermo has developed many unique street foods. Among them are chickpea flour fritters (*panelle*), bread with spleen (*pane con la milza*) and *sfincione,* a type of thick pizza topped with onions, bread crumbs and oregano. *Pasta con le sarde* (pasta with fresh sardines; see *Recipes,* p. 49) is a Palermitan specialty that has achieved national and international fame, even though it is rarely found elsewhere. In the Madonie Mountains, where fish were not readily available, *pasta con le sarde a mare* ("pasta with sardines in the sea") was invented. It has the same ingredients except for the fish!

One of the traditional foods sold in the streets of Palermo for the feast of its patron saint, St. Rosalia, (July 13–15th) are land snails, *babbaluci* in Sicilian, or *vavaluci,* a word that apparently comes from the Arabic and Persian *babbuch,* "curly-toed slippers" (although some think the word derives from *bava lucido,* "shining slime"). There are several kinds of land snails, each with a different name, according to size and color: *babbaluci* are the smallest, *vaccareddi* and *intuppateddi* (also called *favalucieddi* or *scauzzi,* respectively, in southeastern Sicily) are a bit bigger, and *crastuna,* similar to French escargots, are the largest. Land snails (*lumache* in Italian) are popular in Sicily, where many people go snail hunting in the country, especially after a rain. The moisture stimulates dormant snails to eat the parchment-like membrane that seals them inside their shells, so they can emerge to feed. In fact, the Sicilian word *intuppateddi* means "sealed." Snails are also sold in the historical markets. To become edible, the snails must graze on bread crumbs for three days and then soak in water for a few hours. They are cooked and then individually taken out of their shells and eaten with toothpicks.

On St. Lucy's Day (December 13th) Palermitans traditionally don't eat any flour products such as pasta or bread. Instead they eat rice, potatoes or the traditional *cuccìa,* which is prepared by mixing whole wheat berries with fresh, sweet ricotta cheese or with *biancomangiare* (blancmange). Tradition commemorates the 17th century arrival in Palermo Harbor of a ship carrying a load of wheat. Starving Palermitans could not wait for the wheat to be milled and ate the whole wheat berries. In some areas of the interior of the island, wheat berries are eaten in a simple soup, and some towns of the province of Trapani prepare *cuccìa* with cooked wine (*vino cotto*). *Cuccìa* is also popular elsewhere in the island, particularly in the province of Syracuse, where St. Lucy is the patron saint.

Legumes have a special place in culinary traditions throughout Italy, because they provided protein when

Land snails of various sizes are collected in the countryside and sold in historical markets.

meat was rare and present only on the tables of the rich. In the province of Palermo, a very small type of lentil from the island of Ustica and a variety of bean (*fagioli badda*) from the town of Polizzi Generosa have recently gained special recognition from the Slow Food International Movement.

Although pizza is said to have been born in Naples, many variations with different styles of crust, toppings, coverings and fillings have developed elsewhere. *Infriulata* is a type of pizza from the town of Ciminna in the province of Palermo. *Fuazza, impignolata, impanata* and *cudduruni,* available in the province of Agrigento, are other examples.

Artichokes from Cerda, medlars from Trabia and strawberries (*fragoline*) and oranges from Ribera are farm products famous all over the island. *Fragoline* are as small as wild strawberries, and were the only strawberries available in Sicily until about 30 years ago. A unique product harvested in a limited area around the Madonie Mountains today is *manna,* a resinous substance that oozes from the trunk of the ash tree (*Fraxinus fraxinus*) where it is wounded with a special knife. The resin is blue when it first appears, but then turns white with exposure to the air. *Manna* was used as a natural sweetener long ago, and today is produced and used as a sugar substitute in some local products, particularly around the town of Castelbuono. It recently received a special recognition from the Slow Food International Movement. Before the introduction of sugar by the Arabs in the 9th century, honey was the primary sweetener, and it remains an important product in Sicily, especially in the Etna region and southeastern Sicily.

Fiore sicano, a soft cheese with a flavor-producing mold in the rind, is produced in the towns of Castronovo, Cammarata and Santo Stefano di Quisquina, in the area around the Sicani Mountains. *Vastedda del Belice,* the only sheep's milk cheese that is worked into strings or threads, is produced in several towns in western Sicily. These are two of the rarest and very best cheeses in Sicily.

Central Sicily (Enna and Caltanissetta)

Central Sicily preserves some real relics, such as the *vastedda cu sammucu,* a round pizza typical of the town of Troina, layered inside with cheese and salami, and flavored with flowers from the elder tree (*Sambucus nigra*) inside the dough and on top. *Infigghiulata* is another traditional pizza from the Enna and Ragusa provinces, filled with tomato, onions, sliced dry sausage and ricotta cheese, and folded four times using a process called *agnutticcamento.*

Each layer is covered with the same ingredients, and in the end it acquires a rectangular shape.

Piacentino is a saffron-flavored sheep's milk cheese produced in the province of Enna, especially in Piazza Armerina. It has nothing to do with the similarly named northern city of Piacenza; rather, the name may come from the verb *piacere* (to like). The towns of Aidone, Piazza Armerina and Nicosia were founded by northern people who came to Sicily in the 12th century with the Normans, and people still speak a Lombard dialect there. That is why they eat *polenta con cicerchie,* a northern Italian dish, which is made, not from cornmeal, but from a flour ground from a rare kind of beans called *cicerchie.*

As in the rest of Sicily, the local specialties include a seemingly endless variety of sweets. Agira's special almond *cassatelle,* Enna's lemon- and cinnamon-flavored black and white *napolis,* Troina's *infasciateddi,* sweetened and brushed with prickly pear juice, are only a few examples of the astonishing variety of *dolci* that are available only locally. The city of Caltanissetta contributes to the list with a delicious *rollò di ricotta,* and its *torrone* (nougat) is famous all over the island. Delia's *cuddrireddre,* recently saved from extinction by the Slow Food International Movement, deserves special mention for its delicious cinnamon flavor and elaborately twisted shape. *Cuddrireddre* (and many other cognate names of round sweets) comes from the ancient Greek word *kollura* ("round cake").

Eastern Sicily (Messina and Catania)

While Trapani specializes in tuna fishing and cooking, Messina's specialty is the swordfish that go through the strait separating the northeastern tip of Sicily from the mainland. Messina's fishmongers have developed special skill in cutting it into very thin slices, ready to be prepared as swordfish rolls (*involtini di pesce spada*).

In Novara and a few other towns up in the Peloritani Mountains it is possible to find *maiorchino,* a rare and very special cheese prepared with half sheep's milk and half goat's milk. Novara even has a Carnival *maiorchino* festival when big wheels of this cheese are rolled down the streets.

Lately, due to the lack of predators, the number of wild boars (*cinghiali*) has grown rapidly in Sicily. The boars damage forests and nature parks all over the island. In some areas they are now legally hunted and, especially in the Nebrodi Mountains in the province of Messina, their meat is used for

Cuddrireddre, crunchy, fried sweets flavored with cinnamon, orange peel and red wine. Their elaborate crown shape is formed from a long roll of dough.

products such as sausage and salami (*salame di cinghiale*). Boars also are bred on some Sicilian mountain farms, and boar's meat is increasingly present in dishes such as braised boar's meat (*braciole di cinghiale*) and sauces such as boar ragout (*ragù di cinghiale*). Black pigs, now bred on farms in many parts of Sicily, are native to the Nebrodi Mountains. Their meat is used in several different products, such as black pig salami (*salame di maiale nero*).

Mountainous areas are often combed by people in search of wild mushrooms (*funghi*), an extremely popular pastime, especially in northern Italy, but one that can be quite dangerous to people not trained to recognize the poisonous kinds. In Sicily a very good edible wild mushroom grows under the broad leaves of the ferule plant (*Ferula communis*; *ferla* or *ferola* in Italian) and thus is called *funghi di ferla*.

Capers are cultivated on some of Sicily's smaller islands, especially Salina in the Aeolian Islands and Pantelleria to the southwest. Capers are the flower buds, but the *cucunci,* the fruit the plant produces if its beautiful white blossoms are allowed to bloom, can also be eaten, and they have recently gained a special recognition from the Slow Food International Movement. The cuisine of the Aeolian Islands (north of Messina), where capers are one of the main local products, uses *cucunci* extensively and even has a pasta dish with *cucunci* (*pasta alla cucunciata*). A refreshing sweet white dessert wine, *malvasia,* is another product of the Aeolian Islands.

The city and province of Catania have many local pizzas, including *scacce, cartocciate* and *impanate*. The Catanese are very fond of *zuzzu* (butcher's pork scraps cut into small pieces, put into gelatin and cut into squares) and of *masculini,* a fried fish similar to anchovies. They believe *masculini* are much tastier if they have been caught with a trawling net (*pesca di tratta*), which results in removal of part of the gills, and they are willing to pay a premium for fish caught by this method. Ambitious but unscrupulous Palermitan fishmongers will sometimes remove the gills from their catch by hand, then drive three hours to Catania to sell their high-priced fish to the Catanese, who are fooled into believing they were caught with a trawling net.

The egg, a universal fertility symbol, is a ubiquitous Easter icon in Italy. Today Easter eggs are mostly made of chocolate. But Easter cakes baked with hard-boiled eggs (complete with shells) inside are still made in many Sicilian towns and villages, which have their own characteristic designs. Some well-known types are the elaborate *panarieddi* ("little baskets") in Caltagirone and *cuddura cull'ova,* a round cake with eggs inside, from Catania.

Sicilian pistachios, grown on the slopes of Mt. Etna in a limited area around the town of Bronte, are among the best in the world. They recently received a special recognition from the Slow Food International Movement. Culinary innovations using Bronte pistachios include very successful pestos, excellent for dressing pasta. Some examples are *spaghetti con pesto di pistacchio* and *pennette con pesto di pistacchio e mandorle,* for which a recipe is provided on p. 45.

Southeastern Sicily (Syracuse and Ragusa)

Southeastern Sicily preserves its unique character, and here you will find some of the most beautiful and picturesque Sicilian towns. Ragusa Ibla, Noto, Palazzolo Acreide and Modica are real jewels, rebuilt in baroque style after a tremendous earthquake destroyed them in 1693. Many buildings in this area have become UNESCO World Heritage Sites.

The cuisine of the area typically offers pork dishes, especially common in the town of Chiaramonte Gulfi, which specializes in stuffed pork chops (*costata di maiale ripiena,* or *cuoste chini* in Sicilian). Modica is famous for its chocolate and its sweets, which include the very unusual *impanatigghi,* stuffed with chocolate and ground beef. Fava beans have been an important staple on the island for centuries. They are eaten dry in a winter soup called *maccu* (see *Recipes,* p. 46), or fresh in the spring, in dishes such as *frittella* and *fave fresche in umido* (see *Recipes,* p. 63). Modica has a local variety of fava beans (*fave cottoie*) that are eaten with a very large type of handmade fresh pasta (*lolli*) in the dish *lolli con le fave.*

Eels used to be common in all Sicilian rivers. In the old days eels were caught by peasants with handmade traps (*nasse*), similar to lobster traps, and an urticant plant (euphorbia) was often put in the water to lure eels out of their dens to the surface. Today eels caught in the Biviere, a large man-made pond used for hatching fish near Lentini, are still grilled or stewed in a local restaurant.

The carob tree is common in Sicily, especially in the flat highlands of the province of Ragusa. Its large brown pods were eaten in times of war and famine, and its seeds are so regular in weight that they were once used to weigh gold. As in ancient Roman times, carob pods are still used to make a syrup used as a honey or sugar substitute. Other famous products from this area are cherry tomatoes from Pachino and almonds from the towns of Noto and Avola, both of which have received special recognition from the Slow Food International Movement.

Unlike pecorino, which is produced from sheep's (*pecora*) milk, *caciocavallo* is made from cow's milk; its name ("cheese horse") may come from the old custom of hanging cheese pieces tied in pairs over a horse's saddle. One of the best *caciocavallo* cheeses in Sicily is produced in the province of Ragusa and it is called simply *ragusano*. As in the rest of Sicily, fresh ricotta is a delicious, highly perishable by-product of sheep's milk cheese, which is at its best in the winter when Sicily is green and animals have

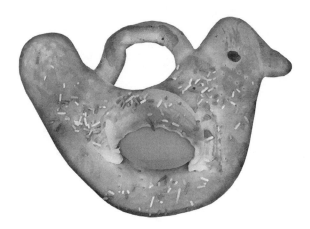

Traditional Easter cookie baked with a hard-boiled egg inside. This type, called *panarieddu*, "little basket" in Sicilian, is made in Caltagirone.

plenty of grass to eat. In some towns of southeastern Sicily it is still possible to meet a shepherd selling his ricotta in *cavagne,* small containers made of canes and tied with rush leaves.

Geography and tradition have conspired to preserve the unique character of local Sicilian foodways. Although each town and city may have a signature cheese, pizza, or style of sweet, they share in common a reverence for fresh ingredients. Sicilians cherish fresh bread, cheese, fish, pasta, vegetables, fruits and espresso, and visitors will surely taste the difference!

Tastes of Sicily

You are encouraged to prepare some of these delicious recipes before leaving home. This is a wonderful and immediately satisfying way to preview the extraordinary cuisine of Sicily. Most recipes are for traditional Sicilian dishes, but a few are examples of nouvelle cuisine, which illustrate how Sicilian chefs today are cooking with classic Sicilian ingredients in a new way. Most of the special ingredients needed to make the dishes can be obtained in the United States in Italian and specialty food markets, or can be ordered (see *Resources, p. 73*). Satisfactory substitutes are given for those that are unavailable.

ANTIPASTI

Tortini ai Porcini

Porcini mushroom tarts. Makes 4.

This recipe was contributed by Giuseppe Carollo, chef and owner of Hostaria Nangalarruni in Castelbuono, which specializes in wild mushroom dishes. Chef Carollo is an experienced mushroom hunter, who began learning the art from his father as a young boy. He avidly hunts wild mushrooms in the woodlands of the Madonie region in the province of Palermo, home to over one thousand varieties.

Vegetable broth

½ CUP ONION, COARSELY CHOPPED

1 MEDIUM CARROT, COARSELY CHOPPED

2 STALKS CELERY, COARSELY CHOPPED

½ TEASPOON SALT

4½ CUPS WATER

Tart

2 MEDIUM POTATOES

½ TEASPOON SALT

¼ TEASPOON PEPPER

[Tortini ai Porcini, *continued*]

 2 LARGE, FRESH PORCINI MUSHROOM CAPS, 3 OUNCES EACH
  AND ABOUT 4 INCHES IN DIAMETER*

 5 TABLESPOONS OLIVE OIL

 2 LARGE SCALLIONS, SLICED

 ¼ CUP VEGETABLE BROTH

 SALT AND PEPPER TO TASTE

 1½ CUPS FRESH, WHOLE-MILK RICOTTA CHEESE

 Garnish

 ¼ CUP FRESH, WHOLE-MILK RICOTTA CHEESE

 2 TABLESPOONS VEGETABLE BROTH

 4 BROCCOLI LEAVES

 4 COOKED BROCCOLI FLORETS

To make broth, add onion, carrot, celery and salt to water in a large pot. Gently boil, partially covered, over medium-low heat. Use broth to make the tart and garnish as noted in the recipe. While broth is cooking, boil whole potatoes until tender. Peel, rice and fork-mash potatoes with salt and pepper until smooth. Set aside. Cut four ¼-inch slices from the center of each mushroom cap and coarsely chop remainder. Brown mushroom slices over medium-low heat in 4 tablespoons olive oil. Remove from pan and drain. Add scallions to the same pan and oil, and sauté over medium heat until limp and lightly brown. Add chopped mushrooms and one tablespoon of olive oil, and sauté until mushrooms are soft and light brown, about 10–15 minutes, stirring frequently. Add ¼ cup of the broth, and salt and pepper to taste. Cook over low heat for about 5 minutes. Add 1¼ cups of the mashed potatoes and blend well. Remove pan from heat. Stir in cheese and mix well. Set aside.

Prepare a non-stick muffin pan with large (approximately ¾-cup) wells. Lightly butter four wells and coat with bread crumbs. Arrange two fried mushroom slices at right angles to each other at the bottom of each prepared well. Fill wells with the mushroom, potato and cheese mixture. Place muffin pan inside a 9" × 13" cake pan. Carefully pour cold water into the cake pan so that the water is about ½ inch below the top of the muffin pan. Bake for 25 minutes at 350°F. Remove muffin pan from cake pan. Invert a cookie sheet over the muffin pan and turn muffin pan upside down. Tarts will slip out of the muffin pan onto the cookie sheet. Use a spatula to transfer tarts to the center of individual plates.

Prepare ricotta cream for garnish. In a small pan, bring cheese and broth to a gentle boil and cook for 2–3 minutes, stirring constantly. The mixture will thicken slightly. Place a dollop on each plate, garnish with a broccoli leaf and floret on top and serve immediately.

*Fresh portabella mushrooms can be substituted for porcini mushrooms.

Arance alla Sagra di Ribera

Oranges in the style of Ribera's festival. Serves 4.

This recipe was provided by Salvatore (Totò) and Vittorio Collura, who in 1990 took over the restaurant business started by their parents in 1981. Their popular Ristorante Leon d'Oro, in the city of San Leone in the province of Agrigento, specializes in fish dishes. The city of Ribera in Agrigento is famous for its sweet oranges. Note: the garlic-infused olive oil needs to be prepared three days ahead of time.

1 WHOLE GARLIC CLOVE

2½ TABLESPOONS EXTRA VIRGIN OLIVE OIL

4 LARGE ORANGES

5 TABLESPOONS SLICED ALMONDS, OVEN-TOASTED

1 SHALLOT, FINELY JULIENNED

HONEY TO TASTE

SALT AND PEPPER TO TASTE

2 TEASPOONS FRESH ORANGE PEEL (SEE INSTRUCTIONS BELOW)

½ CUP BREAD CRUMBS

12 FRESH MUSSELS

1 POUND FRESH, UNCOOKED, PEELED AND DEVEINED SHRIMP*

12 FRESH ORANGE LEAVES

Immerse garlic in olive oil and let sit, covered, at room temperature for three days. Discard garlic after the infusion is completed.

Cut oranges in half, crosswise. Carefully cut around the rim between the segments and the rind. Scoop out the contents so the segments are not broken further. Peel away and discard any large pieces of rind still attached to the segments. Separate segments and chop into ½-inch lengths. Mix with 4 tablespoons almonds, shallot, a drizzle of honey, and salt and pepper to taste. Set aside. Reserve four empty orange halves for the filling. Use a zester to obtain strips of peel from one of the extra orange halves and chop into fine pieces. Mix peel with the olive oil and bread crumbs. Set mixture aside.

Boil mussels until open, about 1 minute. Pry halves apart and discard empty half shells. Heap some bread-crumb mixture into the remaining half shells and brown in the oven at 400°F for about 4 minutes. Set aside and keep warm. In a medium saucepan, bring salted water to a boil and add shrimp. Cook for 1 minute. Drain well and add to orange filling. Heap filling in reserved orange halves and plate individually. Surround filled orange halves with three leaves (orange leaves are ideal, but spinach, endive or Bibb lettuce leaves are fine) and place one filled mussel shell on each leaf. Sprinkle with remaining sliced almonds and serve immediately.

*A count of 40–44 shrimp per pound will provide shrimp of a suitable size for this dish.

Carpaccio di Zucchine

Marinated, thinly sliced zucchini. Serves 4.

The recipe for this side dish was provided by Annamaria Simili, chef and cooking instructor at Azienda Agricola Trinità in Mascalucia, an *agriturismo* or rural B&B located on the eastern slope of Mt. Etna in Catania Province. The Azienda Agricola Trinità includes an organic farm and orchard.

2 ZUCCHINI, ABOUT 8 INCHES LONG

¼ TEASPOON SALT, OR TO TASTE

3 TABLESPOONS OLIVE OIL

2 TABLESPOONS FRESHLY SQUEEZED LEMON JUICE

2 TEASPOONS FRESH MINT (USE SMALL, WHOLE LEAVES)

SPRIG OF MINT FOR GARNISH

Trim ends of zucchini. Use a cheese plane to slice the zucchini lengthwise, discarding the first and last slices. Put slices in a bowl and sprinkle with salt. Blend together olive oil and lemon juice, and gently mix with the zucchini. Stir in mint. Marinate for 15 minutes and then stir again. Garnish with a sprig of mint and serve immediately.

PRIMI PIATTI

Bucatini Freschi con Pesto di Olive

Sicilian olive pesto with currants and raisins over fresh bucatini. Serves 6.

This recipe, developed by Chef Matt Pratt from RP's Fork & Spoon Café, was provided by Peter Robertson, president of RP's Pasta Company in Madison, Wisconsin, maker of traditional fresh Italian pasta using a labor-intensive hand-rolled process. The dish uses *bucatini,* a long pasta with a thin hole down the center.

Olive pesto

6 TABLESPOONS OLIVE OIL

¾ POUND PITTED SICILIAN BLACK OLIVES

¾ CUP SHELLED PISTACHIOS

JUICE AND ZEST FROM 1 ORANGE

¼ TEASPOON CLOVES

1 TEASPOON ANISEED

¼ TEASPOON GROUND CINNAMON

2 DRIED WHITE FIGS, CUT INTO QUARTERS

Currant and raisin sauce

½ CUP SHALLOTS OR ONION, FINELY CHOPPED

½ CUP DRIED CURRANTS

¼ CUP RAISINS

2 CUPS WATER

¼ CUP PINE NUTS

¼ TEASPOON SAFFRON THREADS

½ CUP OLIVE OIL

SALT TO TASTE

1½ POUNDS RP's PASTA FRESH *BUCATINI**

PECORINO CHEESE, FRESHLY GRATED (OPTIONAL)

To make the olive pesto, heat a sauté pan over medium-high heat. Add 2 tablespoons olive oil, olives, pistachios, orange zest, cloves, aniseed and cinnamon. Heat gently until the spices release their perfume and the pistachios toast lightly. Add figs and orange juice, and remove pan from heat. Allow the figs to plump for 5 minutes. Process mixture in a food processor while drizzling in the remaining olive oil until the pesto reaches a good consistency to coat the pasta. Keep mixture warm.

To make the currant and raisin sauce, sauté the shallots in 2 tablespoons olive oil until softened. Add the remaining ingredients and simmer until reduced to a sauce-like consistency that will nicely coat the pasta. Set aside and keep warm.

Bring 6 quarts of water and 1½ tablespoons salt to a rolling boil. Loosen pasta so it doesn't stick together, and add it to the water. Boil for 5–7 minutes until tender, stirring well for the first minute. Drain (do not rinse) and toss with the pesto and currant sauce. Serve immediately and top with freshly grated pecorino.

*See *Resources*, p. 73, for sources of fresh *bucatini*.

Pennette con Pesto di Pistacchio e Mandorle

Small penne with a pesto of pistachios, almonds and basil. Serves 4.

This recipe was provided by Giovanni Farruggio, chef at the Ristorante La Pigna in the Hotel Villa Paradiso dell'Etna in San Giovanni La Punta in the province of Catania. The hotel has remained family-owned since it was built in 1929, but was briefly taken over as an operations center for the German army under General Rommel during WWII. The current owner, Mariagrazia Monaco Rendo, has maintained her family's tradition of fine hospitality and dining.

12 OUNCES *PENNETTE**

⅓ CUP SHELLED PISTACHIOS

½ CUP SLICED ALMONDS

[Pennette con Pesto di Pistacchio e Mandorle, *continued*]

> 5 FRESH BASIL LEAVES, WASHED AND TRIMMED
>
> 3–4 TABLESPOONS OLIVE OIL
>
> ¼ TEASPOON SALT, OR TO TASTE
>
> GROUND PISTACHIOS FOR GARNISH
>
> SMALL SPRIG FENNEL FOR GARNISH†

Cook pasta al dente in salted boiling water. While pasta is cooking, grind pistachios, almonds and basil together with salt and one tablespoon olive oil in a small food processor. The nuts should be in small pieces, not a paste. In a frying pan, warm the nut mixture in the remaining olive oil over low heat. Drain cooked pasta well and stir in nut mixture until all of the pasta is coated. Top with a sprinkle of ground pistachios and a sprig of fennel, and serve.

*Pennette is a smaller version of penne, a straight, quill-shaped tubular pasta, which can be substituted.

†Sicilians use wild mountain fennel, which produces fronds, but not bulbs.

Macco (Maccu)

Dried fava bean purée or thick soup. Serves 4.

This recipe is reprinted with permission from Anna Tasca Lanza from her book, *Flavors of Sicily: The Stories, Traditions and Recipes for Warm-Weather Cooking,* published by Clarkson Potter, Inc., 1996. Anna conducts cooking classes at Regaleali, her family's large country estate near the little village of Vallelunga in central Sicily. The extensive vineyards of the estate produce some of Sicily's most notable wines.

> 2 CUPS DRIED, SKINNED FAVA BEANS*
>
> 1 MEDIUM RED ONION, COARSELY CHOPPED
>
> 1 CUP CHOPPED WILD FENNEL FRONDS OR ½ CUP CHOPPED DILL†
>
> 1 TEASPOON SUN-DRIED TOMATO PASTE DISSOLVED IN ¼ CUP WATER
>
> SALT TO TASTE
>
> FRESHLY GROUND BLACK PEPPER TO TASTE
>
> ¼ CUP OLIVE OIL
>
> 1 CUP TOASTED BREAD CUBES

Soak beans overnight in cold water. Drain and place in a pot with fresh water to cover. Pick out and discard any pieces of skin. Add onion, fennel and dissolved tomato paste, and bring to a boil. Reduce heat and simmer, partly covered, until the beans disintegrate into a soft purée, at least an hour. As the mixture thickens, stir more frequently. Season to taste with salt and pepper, drizzle with olive oil and cool to room temperature. Serve in individual bowls with toasted bread cubes.

*If skinned, dried beans cannot be found, simmer whole dried beans until they soften, about 45 minutes. Squeeze out the beans as you would squeeze roasted garlic, discard skins and continue to simmer until they melt to a soft purée.

†Ordinary fennel fronds are much less flavorful than those from wild Sicilian fennel (*finocchietto*). Dill is sometimes used as an alternative.

Cavati con Seppie e Pistacchi di Bronte

Pasta with cuttlefish and pistachios on a bed of cuttlefish ink. Serves 2.

This recipe was provided by Giovanni Guarneri, chef, sommelier and owner of Ristorante Don Camillo in Syracuse. Chef Guarneri, originally from Palermo, opened the restaurant in 1985 and is noted for his award-winning specialty seafood dishes. The area surrounding Bronte, a city on the western slopes of Mt. Etna, produces 90% of Italy's pistachios.

Tomato sauce

2 POUNDS RIPE TOMATOES, CUT INTO CHUNKS

1 MEDIUM ONION, CUT INTO CHUNKS

8 FRESH BASIL LEAVES

2 TABLESPOONS OLIVE OIL

SALT AND PEPPER TO TASTE

Cuttlefish and pasta

2 CUTTLEFISH (OR SQUID) ABOUT 5–6 INCHES LONG AFTER THE TENTACLES
    ARE REMOVED

4 TABLESPOONS OLIVE OIL

½ CUP MINCED ONION

½ CUP WHITE WINE

SALT AND FRESHLY GROUND PEPPER TO TASTE

3 OUNCES ROASTED PISTACHIOS, COARSELY GROUND

6 OUNCES *CAVATI**

Cuttlefish ink sauce

1 TABLESPOON CUTTLEFISH (OR SQUID) INK

1 TABLESPOON OLIVE OIL

1 CUP TOMATO SAUCE (RECIPE ABOVE)

[Cavati con Seppie e Pistacchi di Bronte, *continued*]

FRESHLY GROUND PEPPER TO TASTE

½ CUP WHITE WINE

SALT (OPTIONAL)

1 TABLESPOON ROASTED PISTACHIOS, COARSELY GROUND

To make the tomato sauce, bring the ingredients to a boil in a saucepan over high heat. Reduce heat and simmer, covered, about 20 minutes, stirring mixture and mashing tomatoes frequently. Add a little water if necessary. Remove from heat and pass mixture through a food mill to purée it and remove tomato skins and seeds. Set sauce aside and keep warm.

Julienne cuttlefish into strips about ¼ inch wide and 3 inches long. Heat olive oil in a frying pan over medium-high heat. Add onion and sauté until limp, about 2 minutes. Add cuttlefish and sauté for 1–2 minutes. Mix in wine and salt and pepper to taste, and cook for 1–2 minutes. Add pistachios and cook for an additional 4 minutes. Set aside and keep warm. Cook pasta al dente in abundantly salted water. Drain and reserve some of the water. Stir pasta into the squid and pistachio mixture. Add a little pasta cooking water if too dry.

In a small saucepan blend together cuttlefish ink, tomato sauce, olive oil, wine and freshly ground pepper to taste. Cook over medium heat to thicken the sauce.

To serve each portion, spoon half the cuttlefish ink sauce in a neat circle at the center of large, light-colored plate. Cover the sauce with half the cuttlefish and pasta mixture. Garnish with ground pistachios and serve immediately.

Cavati are similar in shape and size to small pasta shells, which can be substituted.

Pasta con il Broccolo in Tegame

Pasta and cauliflower cooked in a two-handled pan (tegame). Serves 6.

This recipe was provided by Saverio Patti, a native of Palermo. He is a chef at Agriturismo Antica Stazione Ferroviaria in Ficuzza and an instructor at the Francesco Paolo Cascino Hotel School in Palermo. This is a typical, simple, countryside dish. In Sicily, *broccolo* (pl. *broccoli*) often refers to cauliflower, not broccoli, which is called *sparacelli*.

1¾ POUND HEAD OF GREEN CAULIFLOWER, CUT INTO FLORETS*

5 SCALLIONS, CHOPPED

OLIVE OIL

1 OUNCE ANCHOVIES, PACKED IN OIL (ABOUT FOUR PIECES)

1 TABLESPOON DRIED BLACK CURRANTS

1 TABLESPOON PINE NUTS

SALT TO TASTE

PINCH OF SAFFRON THREADS

¾ POUND *BUCATINI* (DO NOT BREAK INTO SHORTER PIECES)†

1 CUP FRESH RICOTTA CHEESE FROM WHOLE MILK

FRESHLY GROUND BLACK PEPPER TO TASTE

Have two large pots of salted water boiling gently. Add cauliflower to one pot. While cauliflower is cooking, fry scallions in 2–3 tablespoons olive oil in a large frying pan (or a *tegame*) over medium heat until limp. Add ½ cup cauliflower water to the onion mixture. When added water has almost cooked off, add anchovies and break them up with a spoon. The anchovies will "melt" into the liquid. Add pasta to the second pot of boiling water. Drain cauliflower when done (about 5 minutes), reserving remaining cooking water. Add currants, pine nuts, cauliflower and salt to the scallion mixture. Stir well and add saffron. Add ½ cup cauliflower water to pan and break up cauliflower florets with a fork. When pasta is al dente, drain well and add to frying pan. Add more cauliflower water if necessary. Mix together and remove from burner. Add a touch of olive oil and stir in ¾ cup ricotta cheese. Plate individual portions and sprinkle with a little olive oil, freshly ground black pepper and top with remaining ricotta cheese. Serve immediately.

*Green cauliflower is sometimes marketed as carnival cauliflower. It is available at larger supermarkets. White cauliflower heads can be substituted.

†*Bucatini* is a long pasta with a thin hole down the center. It is available at Italian specialty markets and large supermarkets.

Pasta con le Sarde

Pasta with fresh sardines. Serves 4.

This recipe for Sicily's signature dish was contributed by Salvatore Cascino, chef of Ristorante La Botte in Monreale since 1962. The family-owned restaurant offers typical local cuisine in an informal setting.

1 OUNCE DRIED BLACK CURRANTS

10 OUNCES WILD FENNEL FRONDS, WASHED*

6 SCALLIONS, CHOPPED

7 TABLESPOONS OLIVE OIL

2 TABLESPOONS DRY WHITE WINE

12 OUNCES FRESH WHOLE SARDINES, DEBONED AND BUTTERFLIED

3 CANNED ANCHOVIES PACKED IN OLIVE OIL, DRAINED

¼ CUP PINE NUTS

PINCH SAFFRON THREADS (SOAKED IN 2 TABLESPOONS WARM WATER)†

¾ POUND *BUCATINI*††

[Pasta con le Sarde, *continued*]

Soak currants in water until plump. Drain and set aside. Boil fennel in abundant salted water, intact, until tender, about 10 minutes. Coarsely chop and set aside, reserving fennel water for boiling pasta.

Heat 4 tablespoons olive oil in large frying pan. Add three chopped scallions and fry over medium heat until lightly browned. Add 1 tablespoon white wine and cook until it evaporates. Break all but four of the sardines into 2–3 inch pieces. Add the whole sardines and the broken pieces to the pan and fry until fish is flaky, about 2 minutes, being careful to keep the four sardines intact. Set aside and keep warm.

To make the sauce, stir-fry the remaining scallions in another pan over medium heat in 2 tablespoons olive oil until lightly browned. Add remaining wine and cook until wine evaporates. Add fennel, currants, pine nuts and broken sardines. Stir in 1½ cups fennel water, saffron mixture, and salt and pepper to taste. Cook over medium heat for 5–10 minutes. Set sauce aside.

Bring remaining fennel water to a boil. Add pasta and cook al dente. While pasta is cooking, mix anchovies with one tablespoon olive oil in a small saucepan over low heat, mashing and stirring anchovies until they become a smooth paste. Drain pasta well to remove water trapped within it. Stir anchovy mixture into pasta.

To serve, add some sauce to the pasta and blend well. Top with the remaining sauce and decorate each serving with a whole sardine.

*Ordinary fennel fronds can be used, but the flavor will not be as strong.

†Sicilians use a packet of colorant that provides a rich yellow color to many of their dishes, especially those with pasta. We have substituted saffron threads to provide yellow color and saffron taste.

††*Bucatini* is a long pasta with a thin hole down the center.

Cuscus di Pesce

Couscous with fish. Serves 5–6.

Matteo Giurlanda, chef and owner of Ristorante Monte San Giuliano in Erice, provided this delicious recipe. It recalls the Arab contribution to the Sicilian menu. Note that precooked, dried couscous is commercially available. To prepare, follow package instructions, then continue recipe, following last paragraph of instructions.

> *Couscous*
>
> 1 CUP WATER
>
> 1½ TABLESPOONS SALT
>
> 1 POUND DURUM WHEAT SEMOLINA FLOUR
>
> 2 TABLESPOONS OLIVE OIL
>
> *Broth for steaming couscous*
>
> CHEESECLOTH

4 CUPS WATER

1 BAY LEAF

1 TABLESPOON PARSLEY, CHOPPED

½ MEDIUM ONION, COARSELY CHOPPED

½ TEASPOON GROUND CINNAMON

3 CLOVES

½ TEASPOON SALT

Fish broth

3 CLOVES GARLIC, COARSELY CHOPPED

½ MEDIUM ONION, COARSELY CHOPPED

¼ CUP OLIVE OIL

5 TABLESPOONS SLICED ALMONDS

1 TABLESPOON COARSELY CHOPPED PARSLEY

1 LARGE TOMATO, PEELED AND COARSELY CHOPPED

8 CUPS WATER

SALT TO TASTE

1½ POUNDS OF TWO DIFFERENT TYPES OF NON-OILY FISH,

    SUCH AS HADDOCK AND TILAPIA, CUT INTO PIECES

Making couscous will take some practice. Mix together water and salt. Place the semolina on a large, round platter with sloping sides and add a trickle of salted water to it. With a circular motion, rake the semolina with your fingers to moisten it evenly and form small, uniform pellets of dough about half the size of a grain of rice. Pellets should be uniformly damp but not wet. Continue moistening and raking the semolina until all flour has been incorporated into small pellets. Use more salted water if necessary. Larger pellets that form can be broken up by hand or by pressing them through a large-holed sieve. Brush olive oil on the couscous with your fingers. Spread it out on a cloth towel on a cookie sheet. Let sit for about 30 minutes.

To steam couscous, use a *couscoussière** or a large pasta pot that has a steamer basket. (A colander can substitute for the steamer basket.) Line the basket with a piece of cheesecloth. Place water, bay leaf, parsley, onion, cinnamon, cloves and salt in pot and bring to a boil, then reduce heat to low. Put steamer basket on top of pot and fill with couscous. Cut off overhanging cheesecloth so it doesn't burn. If necessary, place a thin strip of dough at the junction of the bottom pot and steamer basket to prevent steam from escaping out the side. Steam for about 1½ hours.

While the couscous is steaming, prepare the fish broth. Sauté garlic and onion in olive oil until brown. Add almonds and sauté until they are lightly browned. Add more oil if necessary. Mix in parsley, tomato, water and salt to taste. When the

[Cuscus di Pesce, *continued*]

mixture starts boiling, add fish and gently boil for 30 minutes. Remove fish and keep warm. Put couscous in a bowl and ladle broth over it. Allow the couscous to sit, tightly covered, for 15–30 minutes to absorb the broth. Serve in soup bowls and top with pieces of fish. Offer remaining broth in a separate serving bowl.

*A *couscoussière* is a specialized double boiler with a lid. The lower part is a cooking pot, often rounded on the sides; the upper part is a snug-fitting pot (with a lid) with holes in the bottom to allow steam in.

Tortelli di Fave Cottoie di Modica su Ragù Maiale al Cioccolato

Homemade pasta stuffed with fava bean paste on a bed of pork ragout with bits of chocolate. Serves 5.

This recipe was created by Peppe Barone, chef and owner of Fattoria delle Torri in Modica, a city in the province of Ragusa. It showcases several regional Sicilian ingredients: lean and tender pork from the black pigs of the Nebrodi Forest; a local variety of fava beans; Modican chocolate, a bitter chocolate reflecting the island's period of Spanish rule; and Cerasuolo di Vittoria, a *DOC* wine* produced in the province of Ragusa from red Frappato and Nero d'Avola grapes. Equivalent ingredients available in the United States may be substituted with good results. The recipe requires a pasta maker. The bean filling and meat mixture (without chocolate) may be made a day in advance and refrigerated.

Fava bean filling

6 OUNCES DRIED, SKINNED FAVA BEANS, SOAKED OVERNIGHT IN WATER

½ TEASPOON SALT

1 TABLESPOON OLIVE OIL

2 TABLESPOONS FINELY DICED ONION

½ CARROT, FINELY DICED

½ STALK CELERY, FINELY DICED

Pork ragout

¼ CUP OLIVE OIL

1 STALK CELERY, FINELY DICED

1 LARGE CARROT, FINELY DICED

¾ CUP FINELY DICED ONION

14 OUNCES PORK (BONELESS COUNTRY-STYLE RIBS,

    FOR EXAMPLE), COARSELY MINCED

1 CUP RED WINE

½ TEASPOON FRESH ORANGE ZEST

½ TEASPOON NUTMEG

¼ TEASPOON TURMERIC

1 BAY LEAF

SALT AND PEPPER TO TASTE

1¼ TEASPOONS SHAVED DARK CHOCOLATE (65%–70% CACAO)

Pasta

1 CUP DURUM WHEAT SEMOLINA FLOUR

3 LARGE EGGS

Garnish

1 LEEK

WHITE FLOUR

OLIVE OIL

¼ CUP FRESH CHICORY OR OREGANO LEAVES

SALT TO TASTE

To make the tortelli filling, rinse soaked fava beans and place in a medium-size pan with salt. Add water to a level about 1 inch above the beans. Cook, partially covered, over medium to medium-low heat until beans are tender, about ¾–1 hour. While beans are cooking, heat olive oil in a small frying pan. Add onion, celery and carrots, and fry over medium heat until soft, about 10 minutes. Remove from pan with a slotted spoon and set aside. When beans are done, transfer with a slotted spoon to a small food processor. Reserve the cooking water. Add vegetables to beans and grind to a smooth paste. If paste is too stiff, add a few teaspoons of the reserved cooking water. Put paste in a bowl, cover with plastic wrap and set aside. If prepared a day in advance, refrigerate paste and some of the cooking water. An hour or two before needed, bring paste and cooking water to room temperature. If paste is too stiff, even after stirring, add a few teaspoons warmed cooking liquid and mix well. Do not let the paste get too soft.

To make the pork ragout, heat olive oil in a medium frying pan over medium heat. Add vegetables and cook until soft, about 10 minutes. Add pork and cook on medium-low heat until meat is no longer pink. Add more olive oil if necessary. Add wine, zest and nutmeg, and cook over medium-high heat for 20 minutes to partially reduce the wine, stirring occasionally. Stir in 1½ cups of warm water, turmeric, bay leaf, and salt and pepper to taste. Partially cover pan and simmer on medium-low heat until the cooking juices are about the same depth as the meat, about 1½ hours. Set aside and keep warm. The chocolate will be sprinkled on the meat mixture just before serving.

[Tortelli di Fave Cottoie di Modica su Ragù Maiale al Cioccolato, *continued*]
To make pasta, place semolina in a medium bowl and make a well in the center. Break one egg into the well. Separate the other two eggs. Reserve the whites and add the yolks to the well in the semolina. Stir with a spoon until semolina is uniformly moist. Form dough into a ball and knead about 5 minutes until smooth and elastic. If dough is sticky, sprinkle surface of hands and kneading surface with some semolina flour. Cover dough ball with plastic wrap and rest it for a half hour to an hour. Divide dough in two parts. Run each portion through a pasta maker, making the dough gradually thinner until it is only about 1 millimeter thick. Use a 3½-inch cookie cutter to cut out 20 circles. Place 1 teaspoon of bean paste off-center on each circle. Touch the edges of each circle with a little beaten egg white and fold the dough over the bean paste, pressing the edges together to seal. Bring ends of half circle together and pinch closed. Drop 5–10 *tortelli* into boiling salted water and cook for about 4 minutes. Pasta should still be somewhat firm. Remove with a slotted spoon and drain well. Set aside. Repeat until all the *tortelli* are cooked.

To make garnishes, remove a 3-inch long piece from the middle of the outer layer of the leek. Finely julienne and coat in flour. Fry in hot olive oil until crispy, no more than a few seconds. Drain on a paper towel. Mash the chicory (or oregano) leaves with a little olive oil and salt to make a pesto.

To serve, arrange meat, reheated if necessary, in a strip about 2 inches wide on the plate. Sprinkle a little chocolate on top. Place 4 *tortelli* on the meat, and garnish with leek. Daub some pesto on each side of the strip and serve.

Vino a Denominazione di Origine Controllata (DOC). DOC wines are produced in well-defined regions according to specific rules designed to preserve the traditional wine-making practices of those regions.

Linguine all'Aragosta

Linguine with lobster. Serves 4.

This recipe was provided by Antonio Pedone and Antonio Billeci, co-owners of Trattoria il Delfino in Sferracavallo, a small seaside village north of Palermo. Il Delfino overlooks the Gulf of Palermo and, not surprisingly, serves traditional Sicilian fish and seafood dishes to a well-satisfied clientele.

2–3 TABLESPOONS EXTRA VIRGIN OLIVE OIL

3 CLOVES GARLIC

PINCH CAYENNE PEPPER, OR TO TASTE

14 OUNCES LINGUINE

4 LOBSTER TAILS, 4–5 OUNCES EACH

½ CUP COGNAC

¾ CUP TOMATO SAUCE

¾ CUP FISH STOCK

SALT TO TASTE

CHOPPED PARSLEY FOR GARNISH

Heat olive oil over medium heat in a large, deep, frying pan. Add whole garlic and cayenne pepper. Discard the garlic when browned. Add lobster tails and cook for 2–3 minutes. Add cognac, tomato sauce, fish stock and salt. Lower the heat, partially cover the pan and simmer sauce until cognac evaporates, about 10–15 minutes. Meanwhile, heat abundantly salted water to cook the pasta. When cognac has evaporated, remove lobster tails from pan. Carefully extract the tail meat and discard the shell. Set the tail meat aside and keep warm. In boiling water, cook linguine al dente according to package instructions. Drain and add to sauce, mixing well. Place linguine on a serving platter and top with lobster tails. Garnish with parsley and serve immediately.

SECONDI PIATTI

Il Pollo Marocchino di Giovanna con Purea di Ceci

Giovanna's Moroccan-style chicken with chickpea cream. Serves 4.

This recipe was provided by award-winning cookbook authors Wanda and Giovanna Tornabene, a mother-daughter team of food professionals who run Tenuta Gangivecchio, a country inn and restaurant outside the remote village of Gangi. The property, formerly an abbey founded by Benedictine monks in 1363, has been in the Tornabene family since 1856. This chicken dish reflects the Arabic contribution to the Sicilian table. According to Giovanna Tornabene, Sicilians eschew chicken for the most part, but savvy restaurateurs include some chicken dishes because they know tourists enjoy them.

This dish can be served with white rice or chickpea cream (recipe below). Note that chickpea cream requires preparation in advance.

½ STICK (¼ CUP) BUTTER

1 LARGE ONION, SLICED

2 TEASPOONS GROUND CINNAMON

4 CHICKEN LEGS OR 8 THIGHS, WITH SKIN REMOVED

1 CUP RAISINS OR DRIED BLACK CURRANTS

1 CUP PITTED PRUNES

½ TEASPOON SALT, OR TO TASTE

¼ TEASPOON PEPPER, OR TO TASTE

PINCH SAFFRON THREADS

[Il Pollo Marocchino di Giovanna con Purea di Ceci, *continued*]

Chickpea cream

  1 POUND DRIED CHICKPEAS, SOAKED OVERNIGHT IN AN EXCESS OF WATER
      AND ½ TEASPOON BAKING SODA

  1 LARGE ONION, CHOPPED

  1 TEASPOON SALT

  FRESHLY GROUND PEPPER

  ½ TEASPOON BAKING SODA

  UP TO 1 CUP WHOLE MILK

Melt butter in a large frying pan over low heat. Add onion and cinnamon and increase heat to medium. Sauté onion until limp. Add chicken and fry until golden. Use more butter if necessary. Add 2 cups water to the chicken, cover and cook 20 minutes. Meanwhile, put raisins and prunes in a bowl and cover with water. After the chicken has cooked 20 minutes, add fruit in water. Add water as needed to completely cover the chicken. Add salt, pepper and saffron. Cover and simmer until the chicken is cooked, about an hour. The sauce will have thickened slightly and become colored by the dried fruit. Serve with white rice or chickpea cream.

To make chickpea cream, drain chickpeas and transfer to a large pot of cold water. Add onion, salt, pepper and baking soda. Bring to a boil and simmer for 2–2½ hours, stirring occasionally, until the chickpeas are tender. Drain the soft chickpeas and purée in a blender. Slowly blend in milk until mixture is creamy. Serve hot.

Polpette in Foglia di Limone

Veal meatballs wrapped in lemon leaves. Serves 4.

This recipe was provided by Annamaria Simili, chef and cooking instructor at Azienda Agricola Trinità in Mascalucia, an *agriturismo* or rural B&B located on the eastern slope of Mt. Etna in the province of Catania. The *agriturismo* includes a large lemon orchard, so fresh lemons and lemon leaves are always close at hand.

  12 OUNCES GROUND VEAL

  2 OUNCES BREAD CRUMBS, MOISTENED WITH WATER

  1 EGG

  1 OUNCE GRATED PARMESAN CHEESE

  ZEST OF ONE LEMON

  20 FRESH LEMON LEAVES, 5 INCHES LONG*

  ⅔ CUP DRY WHITE WINE

  4 TABLESPOONS FRESH LEMON JUICE

  5 TABLESPOONS OLIVE OIL

Mix veal, bread crumbs, egg, cheese and zest together in a bowl until well blended. Form walnut-size balls and flatten each into an oval. Wrap a lemon leaf around each oval and secure ends with a toothpick. Sauté in olive oil until exposed meat is lightly browned, about 5 minutes. The leaves will brown at the edges. Add wine, lemon juice and oil, and cook, covered, for 10 minutes. The leaves should not be eaten. *See *Resources,* p. 73, for a source of lemon leaves. Do not substitute *kaffir* lime leaves or leaves from *salal,* the lemon leaf plant.

Involtini di Lampuga

Stuffed fish (mahi-mahi) rolls. Serves 2.

This recipe was provided by Vincenzo Barranco, owner and former chef of the popular Ostaria del Duomo in Cefalù. Mr. Barranco's sons also work in the restaurant: Davide is the chef and Allesio is the maitre d'hotel. The Ostaria del Duomo specializes in seafood dishes and has an enviable location in front of the Duomo.

¾–1 POUND MAHI-MAHI FILLET

6 TABLESPOONS OLIVE OIL

3 TABLESPOONS ONION, CHOPPED

1 TABLESPOON DRIED BLACK CURRANTS

2 TEASPOONS PINE NUTS

⅔ CUP BREAD CRUMBS

SALT TO TASTE

TOOTHPICKS TO SECURE FISH ROLLS

1 CLOVE GARLIC, COARSELY CHOPPED

8–10 CHERRY TOMATOES, QUARTERED

CAPERS FOR GARNISH

CHOPPED PARSLEY FOR GARNISH

Have your fishmonger cut fish on the diagonal every 3 inches to produce thin slices. Gently pound to flatten so each piece is 3" × 4" and about ¼" thick. To make stuffing, heat 3 tablespoons olive oil over medium heat in a small frying pan. Add onion and fry until limp. Add currants and pine nuts and cook for 5 minutes, stirring frequently. Add bread crumbs and salt to taste. Stir well and remove pan from heat. Place about 2 tablespoons of the stuffing in a strip near one of the short edges of each piece of fish. Starting with this end, roll fish around the stuffing and secure each roll with a toothpick. Heat remaining olive oil in a frying pan over medium-high heat. Add garlic and sauté until golden. Add tomatoes. When they soften, mash them gently with a spoon. Add fish rolls and sauté, covered, about 5 minutes or until fish flakes easily, turning rolls occasionally. Remove rolls to a platter and spoon the tomato sauce over the top. Garnish with some capers and parsley. Serve immediately.

Maiale all'Arancia

Orange-flavored pork. Serves 2.

This recipe was provided by Chiara Agnello, owner of Azienda Agricola Fattoria Mosè, an *agriturismo* or rural B&B. The Mosè farm, close to Agrigento in western Sicily, has been run by the same family since the 18th century, and produces organically grown oranges, lemons, pistachios, almonds, olives and seasonal fruits and vegetables. *Maiale all'arancia* is a dish that is served at Fattoria Mosè to showcase the farm's blood oranges.

2 TABLESPOONS OLIVE OIL

1 POUND PORK TENDERLOIN, CUT IN 2 PIECES

¼ CUP ORANGE LIQUEUR

JUICE FROM 4 FRESH BLOOD ORANGES, STRAINED (1½–2 CUPS)*

SALT TO TASTE

Heat olive oil in a heavy, lidded, 2-quart pot over medium-high heat. Brown the meat on all sides in the hot oil and then remove the pot from the heat. Add orange liqueur and cook over medium-low heat for 5 minutes. Mixture will be bubbly and become brown. Pour in enough orange juice to half cover the meat, and salt to taste. Simmer the meat for about 1¼ hours with the lid slightly open, until the sauce is reduced. Remove the meat and cut into ½-inch slices. Arrange slices on a serving dish and mix with sauce.

*Blood oranges have red flesh and dark red juice. When ripe, their skin is reddish.

Bollito con Patate e Zafferano

Boiled beef with potatoes and saffron. Serves 4.

This recipe was provided by Chef Alessandro Arusa from the Trattoria il Maestro del Brodo in Palermo. The restaurant, owned by his father, Bartolo Arusa, has been in operation since 1985 and features this boiled beef dish as a house specialty.

Broth

2 POUNDS BONELESS BEEF RUMP ROAST

1 POUND BEEF SOUP BONES

1 MEDIUM ONION, SLICED

2 CARROTS, DICED

1½ POUNDS CHERRY OR GRAPE TOMATOES, SLICED IN HALF

2–3 STALKS CELERY, SLICED

Potatoes

2–3 PINCHES SAFFRON THREADS*

2 POUNDS SMALL RED POTATOES, UNPEELED

½ TEASPOON SALT, OR TO TASTE

¼ TEASPOON PEPPER, OR TO TASTE

Vegetables

2 TABLESPOONS OLIVE OIL

1 SMALL ONION, CHOPPED

2 CARROTS, DICED

CHOPPED PARSLEY FOR GARNISH

Add beef and bones to a large pot of salted cold water. Bring to a boil and remove scum. When no more scum forms, discard beef bones and add remaining broth ingredients. Cook until meat is tender. Slice meat into four pieces and keep warm. Reserve broth.

Soak saffron in ¼ cup warm water. To cook potatoes, place in cold water with salt and pepper, and bring to a boil. Cook until soft, about 15 minutes. Do not overcook. Drain, peel and slice potatoes. Put in a bowl. Add saffron water with saffron threads and enough broth so potatoes can be gently stirred to become uniformly light yellow. Keep warm.

To cook vegetables, heat olive oil in pan and add onion and carrots. Sauté until the carrots are soft. Combine potatoes with sautéed carrots and onions. To serve, place a slice of meat in each bowl. Top with one fourth of the potato and vegetable mixture and broth. Sprinkle parsley on top and serve immediately.

*Sicilians use a packet of colorant that provides a rich yellow color to many of their dishes. We have substituted saffron to provide yellow color and saffron taste.

Involtini alla Siciliana

Meat rolls grilled on skewers. Serves 6.

This recipe was provided by Mariano Carbonetti, a native of Palermo. He is a chef at Agriturismo Antica Stazione Ferroviaria in Ficuzza and an instructor at the Paolo Borsellino Hotel School in Palermo. *Involtini alla Siciliana* reflects Sicily's Arabic heritage. While Arabs typically use grape leaves to wrap around a filling, Sicilians use slices of meat, fish fillets or even eggplant as wrappers.

6 MEDIUM POTATOES

6 WOODEN SKEWERS, ABOUT 10 INCHES LONG, SOAKED IN WATER

7 TABLESPOONS OLIVE OIL

½ CUP CHOPPED ONIONS

3 OUNCES PROSCIUTTO, FINELY DICED

1½ OUNCES HARD, DRY SALAMI, FINELY DICED

4 TEASPOONS DRIED BLACK CURRANTS

[Involtini alla Siciliana, *continued*]

> 2 TEASPOONS PINE NUTS
>
> ½ CUP TOMATOES, DESEEDED AND FINELY CHOPPED
>
> ¼ CUP WHITE WINE
>
> ½ CUP GRATED, AGED PECORINO CHEESE, WITH OR WITHOUT PEPPERCORNS
>
> 1 EGG, BEATEN
>
> ½ CUP *CACIOCAVALLO* CHEESE, FINELY DICED*
>
> FRESHLY GRATED BLACK PEPPER TO TASTE
>
> 1 POUND BONELESS BEEF TOP ROUND STEAK (A PIECE ABOUT
>
> > 2 INCHES THICK AND 5 INCHES WIDE), CUT INTO 12 SLICES
> >
> > ⅛–¼ INCH THICK
>
> 1¼ CUPS PLAIN BREAD CRUMBS
>
> PINCH OF OREGANO
>
> OLIVE OIL TO MOISTEN BREAD CRUMBS
>
> 30 LARGE BAY LEAVES
>
> 30 PIECES OF ONION, ABOUT 1½ INCHES SQUARE
>
> 6 CHERRY TOMATOES
>
> FRESH ROSEMARY, CHOPPED

Boil potatoes until done but still firm. When cool enough to handle, peel the potatoes and leave them covered in a warm place. Heat 5 tablespoons olive oil in small frying pan. Add onion and cook over medium-low heat until limp. Stir in prosciutto, salami, currants, pine nuts, tomatoes and wine, and cook for 5 minutes. Add bread crumbs and mix well. Turn off burner. Add pecorino cheese and mix well. Transfer mixture from pan to a small bowl. Add egg and mix well. Blend in *caciocavallo* cheese and pepper. Set aside.

Cut each slice of meat in half crosswise to yield 24 pieces about 2" × 2½." Place a piece of meat between sheets of waxed paper and pound with a mallet until it is roughly rectangular and about four inches at the longest point. Form a small portion of the filling into a sausage shape about ¾ inch in diameter and 1 inch shorter than the width of the meat. Place filling parallel to the shorter length of the meat and begin to roll the meat around it. Firmly press the meat that extends beyond the filling over the ends of the filling while continuing to roll the meat completely around the filling. Repeat for the remaining pieces of meat, making a total of 24 meat rolls. Roll meat rolls in some bread crumbs seasoned with a pinch of oregano and moistened with a little olive oil.

To skewer meat rolls (four to a skewer), begin with a piece of onion followed by a bay leaf. Then poke skewer through the middle of a meat roll at right angles to it. Follow with a piece of onion and bay leaf. Repeat until four meat rolls are on each skewer, separated by a piece of onion and a bay leaf. End with a bay leaf and piece of onion.

Brown one skewer of meat rolls at a time in remaining olive oil over medium heat on a griddle. To brown ends, lift and rotate the skewer so one end of the rolls is on the griddle. Finish cooking in an oven at 350°F for 10 minutes. While meat rolls are in the oven, slice potatoes and lightly fry them. Put some potatoes on each plate. Place a skewer of meat rolls on each plate and carefully remove the skewer. Garnish with a cherry tomato. Sprinkle everything with a pinch of rosemary and serve.

*Caciocavallo is a type of cheese called *pasta filata,* which is made by stretching and molding the curds by hand. More-readily available *pasta filata* cheeses such as provolone or mozzarella can be substituted.

CONTORNI

Caponata di Melanzane con Polpo, Mandorle Tostate e Cacao Amaro

Eggplant with octopus, toasted almonds and bitter cocoa. Serves 6–8.

This recipe was provided by Lucia Birrittella, chef and owner of Ristorante Cin Cin in Palermo, which features Sicilian Mediterranean dishes. It is an example of aristocratic Sicilian Baroque cooking, a specialty of the restaurant. Ms. Birrittella offers hands-on cooking classes for small groups with her son, Vincenzo Clemente, also a chef.

4 6-INCH EGGPLANTS, UNPEELED

1 POUND OCTOPUS TENTACLES

2 BAY LEAVES

1 LEMON, CUT IN HALF

1 LARGE WHITE ONION, SLICED VERY THIN

4 TABLESPOONS OLIVE OIL

2 STALKS CELERY, SLICED VERY THIN

2 TABLESPOONS SUGAR

3 TABLESPOONS WHITE VINEGAR

1 TABLESPOON TOMATO PASTE

DASH CAYENNE

OLIVE OIL FOR DEEP-FRYING EGGPLANT

¼ CUP SLICED ALMONDS, TOASTED

2 TEASPOONS POWDERED DARK COCOA

[Caponata di Melanzane con Polpo, Mandorle Tostate e Cacao Amaro, *continued*]
Cut eggplant into 1-inch cubes and place in a bowl. Salt well to draw out juices and let sit for ¾ hour. Place octopus in boiling water for 3–4 minutes. Drain, then scrape off and discard skin. Put octopus in a fresh pot of boiling water with salt, bay leaves and lemon. Boil for about 1 hour until fork-tender. Turn off burner and do not drain. Cook onion in olive oil over low heat, covered. When the lid is lifted, let any condensed water inside lid return to pan. When onion is limp, add celery and cook until tender. Add sugar and mix well. Increase temperature to medium-high to caramelize sugar, and cook about 4 minutes. Add vinegar. The mixture will sputter. Cook until sputtering stops and vinegar burns off, about 2 minutes. Add tomato paste and stir well. Set aside. Rinse eggplant in water. Drain and squeeze gently to remove water. Pat dry with paper towels. Deep-fry eggplant in batches in olive oil. When medium-brown and crispy, remove from oil and drain in a strainer lined with paper towels. Place eggplant on bottom of serving dish. Cut octopus in ½-inch slices and layer on top of eggplant. Cover with hot onion mixture. Sprinkle almonds over onions and dust the top with cocoa. Serve at room temperature. The dish will get mushy if reheated. The dish looks dry when first assembled, but will moisten as the eggplant "weeps."

Foglie Fritte di Carciofi

Fried artichoke leaves. Serves 2.

This recipe was adapted and printed with permission from Catherine Tripalin Murray from her book *Grandmothers of Greenbush: Recipes and Memories of the Old Greenbush Neighborhood,* published by Greenbush...remembered, 1996. It is a dish made by Ms. Murray's grandmother, Caterina DiMaio Tripolino, who arrived in New York City from Sicily in 1910 and settled the following year in Madison, Wisconsin, in the Greenbush neighborhood, the center of the city's Italian community. When Greenbush was destroyed in an urban renewal project in 1960, Ms. Murray preserved its memories in several cookbooks highlighting the culinary history of the old neighborhood.

> 2 LEMONS
>
> 2 ARTICHOKES
>
> 1–2 EGGS, BEATEN
>
> FLOUR FOR DREDGING
>
> CORN OIL FOR DEEP FRYING
>
> SALT AND PEPPER TO TASTE

Squeeze lemons. Add juice and squeezed lemon halves to about a quart of water in a pan or bowl. Carefully snap off and discard outer artichoke leaves until the yellow base can be seen. Cut off the top of the artichoke, leaving about 1½ to 2 inches above the stem. Snap off remaining leaves and place in lemon water to keep them from turning black. (Reserve small, inner leaves and artichoke heart for another use.) Pat leaves dry with paper towels. Dredge in egg, then flour. Sprinkle with salt and pepper, and fry in oil at 360°F until golden brown on both sides. Drain on paper towels in a pan lined with aluminum foil. Cover fried leaves with foil to keep warm until all frying is completed. Serve immediately.

Fave Fresche in Umido

Fresh fava beans with tomato and shallots. Serves 4.

The recipe for this side dish was contributed by Giovanni Matranga from Palermo, who lives in Mondello, a beach resort north of Palermo. Mr. Matranga is a lecturer on the subjects of Sicilian history and politics for Elderhostel programs. He is a retired high school teacher of English and finds cooking to be one of life's great pleasures. His wife, Marcella Croce, is co-author of this guidebook.

4 POUNDS FRESH YOUNG FAVA BEANS IN THE POD*

2 SHALLOTS, CHOPPED

4 CHERRY TOMATOES, CUT IN HALF, OR 1 RIPE TOMATO, CHOPPED

4 TABLESPOON OLIVE OIL

Shell and rinse beans. Stir-fry shallots in olive oil until soft. Add tomato and fry for 1–2 minutes over medium heat. Add beans and cover with water. Season with salt to taste. Boil on low heat for about 20 minutes, or until cooked.

*Fava beans have big, bulky pods, so the beans comprise comparatively little of the total weight. Buy young pods with beans about the size of a small lima bean, as judged by gently feeling the beans within the pods. Beans are connected to the pod through a short, green strip on one edge, which is visible on shelled beans. The strip becomes black in older beans and should be cut away before the beans are cooked.

Caponata con Peperoni

Sweet-and-sour eggplant with red bell pepper. Serves 4.

This recipe was provided by Annamaria Simili, chef and cooking instructor at the agriturismo Azienda Agricola Trinità in Mascalucia (Catania Province). This *agriturismo* (a rural B&B that usually is on a working farm) is owned by her sister-in-law, Marina Bonajuto. One of Sicily's most popular dishes, *caponata* can also include other ingredients, even fish.

SUNFLOWER OIL FOR DEEP-FRYING

2 MEDIUM EGGPLANTS, 1¾ TO 2 POUNDS COMBINED WEIGHT,

UNPEELED AND CUT INTO 1-INCH CUBES.

1 LARGE RED BELL PEPPER, DESEEDED AND CUT INTO 1-INCH PIECES

½ CUP FINELY CHOPPED ONION

[Caponata con Peperoni, *continued*]

1 STALK CELERY, FINELY SLICED

1 TABLESPOON OLIVE OIL

2 TABLESPOONS CAPERS, DRAINED

¼ TEASPOON SALT, OR TO TASTE

2 TABLESPOONS HONEY

6 TABLESPOONS WHITE VINEGAR

Heat sunflower oil over high heat in a large, deep frying pan. Use enough oil to cover the eggplant so that it does not become mushy. Slowly add eggplant to hot oil. Deep-fry until cubes are light brown and crispy, about 12–15 minutes. Remove from oil with a slotted spoon and drain well. Set aside. Add pepper pieces to the same oil and fry about 2–3 minutes over high heat. Remove from oil, drain, pat dry, and set aside with eggplant. Sauté onion and celery in a small frying pan in olive oil over medium heat until onion is translucent. Stir in capers and salt. Transfer onion mixture to a medium-sized frying pan without additional oil. Add eggplant and pepper, and mix well. Stir in honey and vinegar. Cook and stir over medium heat until vinegar evaporates, about 5 minutes. Serve at room temperature.

DOLCI

Dolci del Ragusano

Dessert with cheese from the province of Ragusa. Serves 5–6.

This recipe was provided by Vincenzo Candiano, chef at the lovely Locanda Don Serafino in Ragusa Ibla. Dolci del Ragusano is one of the dishes chef Candiano created to showcase the celebrated Ragusa cheese (*DOP*)*. Chef Candiano prepares a puff pastry (*pasta sfoglia*), which serves as the dessert's base. Making *pasta sfoglia* is a difficult process, so we suggest using sheets of frozen puff pastry. For best results and a richer flavor, the sweet cheese mixture should be prepared about 10 hours before serving.

Sweet cheese mixture

3 EGG YOLKS

6 TABLESPOONS SUGAR

5 TABLESPOONS CORNSTARCH

2⅛ CUPS COLD MILK

2½ OUNCES RAGUSANO CHEESE, THINLY SLICED AND BROKEN INTO PIECES

8 OUNCES WHIPPING CREAM

FROZEN PUFF PASTRY SHEETS

Spun sugar (filo di caramello)

⅔ CUP WATER

2 CUPS SUGAR

2 TABLESPOONS LIGHT CORN SYRUP

THYME-FLAVORED HONEY†

SHORT SPRIGS OF FRESH THYME

To make the sweet cheese mixture, whisk together yolks, sugar and cornstarch in a medium-sized saucepan, then slowly add the milk. Cook over medium heat for 4–5 minutes, whisking constantly. The mixture will thicken very quickly at the end of this time. Add cheese and continue to cook and whisk until cheese is almost melted. Remove from burner and whisk until cheese is fully melted and totally incorporated. Refrigerate on top of a hot pad for 15–20 minutes. While mixture is cooling, whip the cream. When the cheese mixture has cooled sufficiently so that a finger can be comfortably dipped into it, fold in whipped cream and whisk gently until smooth. Refrigerate about 10 hours before use.

Bake puff pastry sheets according to package instructions. Cut out 3" × 4" bases and small triangles for garnishes.

To make spun sugar garnish, add water to a medium-sized saucepan. Slowly add sugar. Drizzle in corn syrup and stir gently to keep sugar from coating sides of pan. Bring to a boil over medium-high heat without stirring. Cover and cook until sugar is dissolved, about 2–3 minutes. Uncover and cook until the mixture is amber-colored, about 7–9 minutes. Remove from burner and swirl mixture to make color uniform. Stop cooking process by briefly plunging pan in ice water. Let caramel mixture stand for 1–2 minutes to cool and thicken. Dip a fork into the mixture and pull it out again until long, fine threads form at the end of the fork tines after the heaviest caramel has fallen off the fork. Pull on the threads and continue to draw off more length with your hands. Shape the threads into a bundle or nest and put on parchment paper. When no more sugar threads can be pulled, dip the fork again, and repeat the process. Strands melt when handled, so touch the bundles as little as possible, and use them immediately.

To serve, place two scoops of creamy cheese mixture on top of a puff pastry base. Top with a thin, short slice of cheese and a small triangle of puff pastry placed at an angle. Drizzle the dessert with some honey, and garnish with a few sprigs of fresh thyme and a bundle or nest of spun sugar.

*Ragusano cheese is an uncooked cheese made from whole cow's milk. *DOP* stands for *Denominazione di Origine Protetta,* "Protected Designation of Origin," a certification that means that the milk used to make the cheese and the methods of its production are traditional to the location and conform to high standards. This cheese is available at Italian markets and at many supermarkets with large delicatessen departments.

†Unflavored honey may be substituted.

Mousse di Ricotta

Ricotta mousse. Makes 3 large or 6 small muffin-sized desserts.

This recipe was contributed by Angelo Treno, chef and owner of Al Fogher, a popular restaurant on the outskirts of Piazza Armerina. Chef Treno is recognized for his mixture of traditional culinary artistry with imaginative nouvelle concepts.

15 OUNCES FRESH RICOTTA CHEESE

HEAPING ¼ CUP SUGAR

6 TABLESPOONS *MOSCATO* WINE (MUSCATEL)*

2 TABLESPOONS FRESH CREAM

1 PACKET UNFLAVORED GELATIN (2¼ TEASPOONS)

1 TABLESPOON HOT WATER

Nut topping

2 OUNCES ALMONDS, COARSELY GROUND

2 OUNCES PISTACHIOS, COARSELY GROUND

2 OUNCES HAZELNUTS, COARSELY GROUND

2 OUNCES PINE NUTS

Caramelized sugar sauce

⅔ CUP SUGAR

2 TABLESPOONS HONEY

2–3 TABLESPOONS WARM WATER

Chocolate sauce

3 OUNCES MILK CHOCOLATE, 40% COCOA MINIMUM

⅔ CUP WATER

1 TEASPOON WILD FENNEL SEEDS, CRUSHED†

Mix together ricotta, sugar and half of the *moscato*. Stir in cream and set aside. To dissolve gelatin put remaining *moscato* in a metal bowl on top of a small saucepan of boiling water just removed from the burner. Add 1 tablespoon hot water. Slowly add gelatin, stirring constantly. When gelatin is dissolved, stir it into the cheese mixture. Spoon into non-stick muffin pans, filling cups to the top. Refrigerate for 3 hours.

Mix the nuts together and toast in the oven at 350°F until lightly brown. Set aside. To prepare the caramelized sugar sauce, melt sugar in a small saucepan over medium-low heat, stirring constantly. When the sugar has caramelized, it will be golden brown and liquid. Remove from the burner and carefully stir in honey and warm water; the mixture will bubble up. To prepare the chocolate syrup, melt chocolate over medium-low heat in ⅔ cup water. Add fennel seeds and strain the sauce to remove any large bits of fennel. To unmold the mousses, first run a knife around the edges of the muffin wells. Then immerse the muffin pan in a shallow hot water bath for about 30 seconds. Overturn a cookie sheet on top of the muffin pan, hold the two together and flip upside down. Transfer each released mousse to a plate. To serve, sprinkle toasted nuts on top. Then drizzle with warm caramelized sugar sauce and chocolate syrup.

*Moscato (muscatel) is a light-amber, sweet dessert wine made from muscat grapes. Sweet Marsala wine can be substituted.

†Wild fennel seeds have more flavor than cultivated fennel seeds, but are not readily available outside of Sicily. Ordinary fennel seeds are a reasonable substitute.

Ripieno per Cannoli

Ricotta filling for cannoli.

This recipe for sweetened ricotta cheese (2½ cups) fills 18 medium cannoli or 36 mini cannoli, crispy fried pastry tubes.*

This recipe was provided by Conchera Capadona, whose parents, Ninfa and Vito Capadona, emigrated from Sicily to Madison, Wisconsin, and in the 1930s opened the first Italian restaurant in the Italian-American Greenbush area. Although this old neighborhood and their original Bunky's restaurant fell victim to an urban renewal project in the 1960s, Conchera's granddaughter, Teresa Pullara-Ouabel, revived the family legacy in 2004. With her Moroccan husband, Rachid Ouabel, Teresa opened Bunky's Cafe, also in Madison, which showcases dishes that combine the flavors of Italian and Mediterranean cuisine.

2 CUPS WHOLE-MILK RICOTTA CHEESE

1 CUP HEAVY CREAM, WHIPPED

3 TABLESPOONS SUGAR

1½ TEASPOONS ALMOND EXTRACT OR 1 TEASPOON VANILLA EXTRACT

¼ CUP CHOPPED SEMISWEET CHOCOLATE OR CHOCOLATE CHIPS

CANDIED FRUIT AND NUTS (OPTIONAL)

Mix ricotta cheese with sugar in a bowl and fold in the whipped cream. Add almond or vanilla extract, chocolate or chopped fruit and nuts, and blend well. Refrigerate for 1–3 hours to set the filling. When ready to serve, fill a pastry bag (or a plastic food storage bag with a corner cut off) with ricotta cream and squeeze it into the open ends of each pastry tube. If the shells are filled too far in advance, the cream will soften the pastry, which is best when crispy. Decorate ends with some chocolate chips, chopped nuts or candied fruit.

*Cannoli pastry tubes or shells are available at Italian food markets. See *Resources,* p. 73, for a mail-order supplier.

Froscia

No-crust Sicilian ricotta pie. Serves 10–12.

This recipe was provided by Giovanna Miceli-Jeffries, a scholar in contemporary Italian narrative and Italian feminist writings and culture, who teaches Italian at the University of Wisconsin–Madison. *Froscia* is a typical Easter-season dessert of Ribera, Dr. Miceli-Jeffries' hometown in the province of Agrigento. According to oral tradition, the dish has humble origins in a quiche-like frittata cooked by shepherds in their fields, using fresh ricotta with eggs and milk, all abundant spring products in Sicily.

> 6 EGGS
>
> 1 CUP SUGAR
>
> ¾ POUND RICOTTA CHEESE
>
> ½ POUND FINELY GRATED PARMESAN CHEESE
>
> 1 CUP MILK
>
> ¾ TEASPOON VANILLA
>
> ¼ TEASPOON CINNAMON
>
> 4 LARGE LEAVES FRESH MINT, FINELY CHOPPED
>
> ¼ CUP FINE WHITE BREAD CRUMBS
>
> 1 TABLESPOON SEMISWEET CHOCOLATE, CHOPPED INTO BITS
>
> OLIVE OIL FOR GREASING PAN

Beat eggs gently until well blended. Stir in sugar. In a separate bowl, slowly stir milk into ricotta. Add to egg mixture and mix well. Gradually add remaining ingredients, stirring well after each addition. Lightly oil sides and bottom of a 9" × 9" cake pan with olive oil. Pour batter into pan and cover with foil. Place in the middle rack of a 375°F oven and bake for 30 minutes. Uncover pan and move it to the upper rack. Continue baking until uniformly golden brown, about 45 minutes longer. Insert a toothpick to check for doneness. The consistency should be that of a rather dry quiche. Serve at room temperature.

Genovesi

Genoa cakes. Makes 8 cakes.

This recipe is reprinted with permission from Mary Taylor Simeti from her book *Bitter Almonds: Recollections and Recipes from a Sicilian Girlhood* written in collaboration with Maria Grammatico and published by Bantam Books, 1994. *Bitter Almonds* tells the story of Ms. Grammatico's early years in a convent-like orphanage in Erice, where she learned to make the exquisite sweets and pastries that she now sells in her Erice pastry shop, the Pasticceria Maria Grammatico.

Pastry cream

1 EGG YOLK

5 TABLESPOONS SUGAR

2 TABLESPOONS CORNSTARCH

1 CUP WHOLE MILK

½ TEASPOON GRATED LEMON ZEST

POWDERED SUGAR FOR DUSTING

Pastry dough

¾ CUPS DURUM WHEAT SEMOLINA FLOUR

1 CUP PLAIN FLOUR

¼ TEASPOON SALT (OPTIONAL)

7 TABLESPOONS SUGAR

3½ OUNCES MARGARINE, CUT INTO PIECES

2 EGG YOLKS

COLD WATER, ABOUT 3–4 TABLESPOONS

To make the pastry cream, whisk together the egg yolks and sugar in a small, heavy saucepan. Dissolve the cornstarch in a quarter of the milk, then gradually add the rest of the milk and mix well. Slowly pour the milk mixture into the egg mixture, whisking until well blended. Cook over low heat for 10–12 minutes, stirring constantly, until shiny and very thick, the consistency of pudding. (Or cook in a double boiler for 20–25 minutes.) Stir in the lemon zest. Pour into a bowl and cover with plastic wrap placed directly on top of the cream. Cool and refrigerate until ready to use. The cream can be refrigerated for up to 3 days. Whisk until smooth if it separates.

To make the pastry dough, process the durum wheat flour in a food processor until fine and silky to the touch, about 5 minutes. Add the plain flour, salt, and sugar and pulse to mix. Add the margarine and process until crumbly. Add the egg yolks, one by one, pulsing to mix. With the processor running, add just enough water so the dough comes away from the sides of the bowl. Too much water will make the dough difficult to work.

Turn dough out onto a floured surface and press together to form a ball. Do not overwork, or the pastry will be tough. Wrap in plastic wrap and refrigerate for at least 30 minutes before rolling out. The dough can be refrigerated for up to 1 week or frozen for up to 1 month.

Preheat oven to 425°F. Divide the dough into 8 pieces. On a floured surface, roll out each piece into a rectangle about 6" × 4" × ³⁄₁₆" thick. Place 2 tablespoons of the cream on one half of each rectangle, fold the other half over, and press the edges together with your fingers. Then cut out circles from the rectangles, using a

[Genovesi, *continued*]

3" round fluted cookie cutter, a drinking glass, or a pastry wheel and place about 1" apart on a baking tray. Bake for 7 minutes, or until lightly browned. Transfer to a rack to cool briefly. Sprinkle with powdered sugar. *Genovesi* are best eaten warm.

Sorbetto di Mandarino

Mandarin orange sorbet. Serves 6.

This recipe was provided by Giusy Costanzo, daughter of the late master ice cream maker, Corrado Costanzo. Ms. Costanzo is carrying on the tradition of her father, who created sublime confections for almost 50 years in his ice cream and pastry shop in Noto, which is named after him, Corrado Costanzo. Mandarin orange sorbet is the shop's signature sorbet and is the most popular variety in the shop.

¼ CUP THICK GLUCOSE SYRUP*

2 CUPS WATER

6 TABLESPOONS LIQUID INVERT SUGAR*

1¼ CUPS GRANULATED TABLE SUGAR

⅓ CUP LEMON JUICE (ABOUT 2 LEMONS)

½ CUP MANDARIN ORANGE JUICE (ABOUT 2 MANDARIN ORANGES)

1 TABLESPOON MANDARIN ORANGE ZEST

⅝ CUP DEXTROSE POWDER†

1 EGG WHITE

Add glucose syrup to water and whisk to blend. Add invert sugar and mix well. Stir in table sugar, lemon juice, mandarin orange juice and zest. Add dextrose and whisk mixture well. To help blend in the egg white, add a ladle or two of the sorbet mixture to the egg white in a bowl. Whisk until blended and add to the sorbet mixture. Filter solution and pour into a 7" × 11" glass dish. Freeze overnight. In the morning, remove from freezer and mash mixture with a wooden spoon to break large ice crystals and form a smooth mixture. Return to freezer and freeze again.

*Available at baking and cake-decorating specialty stores.

†Available at wine- and beer-making specialty stores.

Shopping in Sicily's Food Markets

Helpful Tips

Outdoor Markets

Soaking up culture in the colorful, bustling Sicilian street markets is on every food lover's agenda. Sicily has several spectacular historic markets, which are open daily. Nestled in the old section of some of the larger cities, some old markets have been in existence since the Saracens conquered Sicily in the early 900s. Stalls packed with food and housewares often line both sides of narrow, winding alleyways, shielded from the elements by wide overhead canopies. Also intriguing are the ubiquitous smaller weekly markets that you will undoubtedly encounter serendipitously.

Vendors hover over and hawk tempting mounds of fragrant foods to take home to cook or sample on the spot. The eye is distracted by an unfamiliar item, perhaps some knobby-looking fruit or tuber. Food generally is priced, but not always identified. If you would like to know the name of an item, be prepared to ask, "What is this called?" (see *Helpful Phrases,* p. 77). If you intend to buy, don't haggle too much over the price. It is unlikely you will find cheaper prices or fresher food anywhere.

In their season, expect to find artichokes with deep purple leaves, plump heads of green or even purple cauliflower, smooth, pale-green, cylindrical squash (*zucchina lunga*) that grow 2–3 feet long and sea urchins prized for their tasty orange corals (roe-producing organs) among piles of fresh fish and seafood. For a quick snack in a bun, try fried beef spleen (*milza*) or chickpea fritters (*panelle*), specialities of Palermo.

So many images in the markets beg for photographic capture. Some folks, however, are not comfortable about having their picture taken. Always ask first.

The Indoor Markets

Food sold indoors is more expensive. Stores range from small neighborhood convenience shops to supermarkets with a wide assortment of groceries and non-comestibles. You may be tempted to get the makings for a tasty picnic. Remember to pack some plastic tableware before leaving home!

The following abbreviated list of weights in Italian proved sufficient to get the quantities we wanted. Corresponding approximate weights in ounces are included.

un etto: 100 grams, or about a quarter pound (3.5 ounces)
due etti: 200 grams, or about 7 ounces
mezzo chilo: half kilo, or about one pound (17.5 ounces)

If you are considering bringing food back to the United States, obtain the Customs and Border Protection (CBP) brochure "Know Before You Go" to find out which agricultural items are allowed. The number to call is 1-877-CBP-5511. Listen to the menu and choose the option for ordering brochures. Alternatively, listen to a taped message with the same information. This information can also be found at: http://www.cbp.gov/xp/cgov/travel/vacation/kbyg. Be aware that websites do change, so you may have to go to the CBP homepage (www.cbp.gov) and click on "travel" to get to the page of interest.

A Health Precaution

Don't ask for trouble. Avoid eating food from street vendors. Some serious diseases can be transmitted by eating unclean produce. If you buy fruits and vegetables in the markets, make sure to wash them thoroughly with bottled water before eating. The safest fruits are those that can be peeled. Bottled water is readily available and is a wise choice, even in restaurants. Using bottled water even for tooth brushing is a good way to avoid problems when traveling anywhere.

Resources

Online Suppliers of Sicilian Foods

While many retail sources sell Sicilian/Italian foods, most do not carry the special ingredients required for the recipes in this book. These ingredients are available in Sicilian/Italian food markets, natural and whole food stores, and large supermarkets.

Sicilian/Italian food items also can be purchased online from several websites. Since websites change their addresses, or URLs, and may not be updated regularly, you will probably need to do additional browsing. We suggest that you use your favorite search engine (our standby is google.com) and do a general search for Sicilian/Italian food markets or a specific search for a desired ingredient. We hope the following online businesses continue to offer fine Sicilan/Italian products for our readers.

RP's Pasta Company sells several varieties of fresh pasta, including *bucatini,* a spaghetti-like pasta with a hole (*buco*) down the center, which is used in the recipe they shared with us (see *Recipes,* p. 44). The company's products are available in many stores in the Midwest, and the geographical area it serves is expanding in size. If you want to make fresh pasta or *gnocchi,* their "Ecco La Pasta" product line provides all the ingredients in a bag. Just add water and follow the preparation instructions.

RP's Pasta Company
1133 East Wilson Street
Madison, WI 53703
Tel: 608-257-7216
Fax: 608-257-7267
info@eccolapasta.com
http://www.rpspasta.com

Melissa's / World Variety Produce is one of the largest distributors of specialty produce in the United States. The company imports and distributes exotic fresh fruits and vegetables from around the globe, stocking over 800 different varieties at any given time. Fresh lemon leaves (needed to make the recipe on p. 56) are not listed on the website, but they are available. To order, use Melissa's hotline. Leaves that are 5 inches long work best.

Melissa's / World Variety Produce, Inc.
P.O. Box 21127
Los Angeles, CA 90021
Hotline: 800-588-0151
hotline@melissas.com
http://www.melissas.com

There are six Claro's Italian Markets in southern California. One is listed below. Many of the Italian foods are imported directly from Italy. The company also has a cyberstore. Claro's not only carries cannoli shells, but they sell them by the piece. Many stores require the purchase of a case, or at least many more than are needed. We provide a recipe for cannoli filling (p. 67); this market is a handy resource for the shells.

Claro's Italian Market
714-832-3081
1095 E. Main St.
Tustin, CA 92780
Tel: 800-507-0450 (cyberstore)
http://store.claros.com

Tours and Travel Advice

Marcella Croce (co-author of this guidebook) and her husband Giovanni Matranga have been lecturers and coordinators of the Elderhostel Programs in Sicily for almost 20 years. They are available to help you design your itineraries. They also provide professional guided tours of the city of Palermo and other destinations in western Sicily. They can be contacted at:

marcellacroce@gmail.com

Some Useful Organizations to Know About

Italian Consulate in Chicago

Italian Consulate General
500 North Michigan Ave., Suite 1850
Chicago, IL 60611
Tel: 312-467-1550/1/2
Fax: 312-467-1335
italcons.chicago@esteri.it
http://www.conschicago.esteri.it/Consolato_Chicago

International Organizations

We are supporters of two international organizations that promote good will and understanding between people of different cultures. These organizations, Servas and The Friendship Force, share similar ideals but operate somewhat differently.

Servas

Servas, from the Esperanto word meaning "serve," is a non-profit system of travelers and hosts. Servas members travel independently and make their own contacts with fellow members in other countries, choosing hosts with attributes of interest from membership rosters. It is a wonderful way to get to know people, be invited into their homes as a family member, share experiences and help promote world peace. For more information about membership in Servas, write or call:

United States Servas, Inc.
1125 16th St., Suite 201
Arcata, CA 95521-5585
Tel: 707-825-1714
Fax: 707-825-1762
info@usservas.org
http://www.usservas.org

The Friendship Force

The Friendship Force is a non-profit organization that also fosters good will through encounters between people of different backgrounds. Unlike Servas, Friendship Force members travel in groups to host countries. Both itinerary and travel arrangements are made by a member acting as exchange director. These trips combine stays with a host family and group travel within the host country. For more information on membership in The Friendship Force, write:

The Friendship Force
233 Peachtree St., Suite 2250
Atlanta, GA 30303
Tel: 404-522-9490
Tel: 800-554-6715
Fax: 404-688-6148
ffi@thefriendshipforce.org
http://www.thefriendshipforce.org

Helpful Phrases

For Use in Restaurants and Food Markets

In the Restaurant

The following phrases in Italian will assist you in ordering food, learning more about the dish you ordered, and determining what specialties of a locality are available. Each phrase also is written phonetically to help with pronunciation. Syllables in capital letters are accented. You will discover that Sicilians heartily encourage your attempt to converse with them in Italian. By all means, give it a try at every opportunity.

DO YOU HAVE A MENU?	Ha il menu? *Ah eel meh-NOO?*
MAY I SEE THE MENU, PLEASE?	Posso vedere il menu, per favore? *POH-soh veh-DEH-reh eel meh-NOO, pehr fah-VOH-reh?*
WHAT DO YOU RECOMMEND?	Che cosa consiglia lei? *Keh KOH-sah kohn-SEE-yee-ah LEH-ee?*
DO YOU HAVE . . . HERE? (ADD AN ITEM FROM THE *MENU GUIDE* OR THE *FOODS & FLAVORS GUIDE*.)	Ha . . . in questo ristorante? *Ah . . . een KWEH-stoh reeh-stoh-RAHN-teh?*

HELPFUL PHRASES

RESTAURANT

WHAT IS THE "SPECIAL" FOR TODAY?

Qual è il piatto del giorno?
Kwah-LEH eel pee-AH-toh dehl jee-OHR-noh?

DO YOU HAVE ANY SPECIAL LOCAL DISHES?

Ci sono specialità locali?
Chee SOH-noh speh-chee-ah-lee-TAH loh-KAH-lee?

IS THIS DISH SPICY?

Questo piatto è piccante?
KWEH-stoh pee-AH-toh EH pee-KAHN-teh?

I / WE WOULD LIKE TO ORDER . . .

Vorrei/Vorremmo ordinare . . .
Voh-REH-ee / Voh-REH-moh or-dee-NAH-reh . . .

WHAT ARE THE INGREDIENTS IN THIS DISH?

Quali sono gli ingredienti di questa pietanza?
KWAH-lee SOH-noh yee een-greh-dee-EHN-tee dee KWEH-stah pee-eh-TAHN-zah?

WHAT ARE THE SEASONINGS IN THIS DISH?

Quali sono i condimenti di questa pietanza?
KWAH-lee SOH-noh ee kohn-dee-MEHN-tee dee KWEH-stah pee-eh-TAHN-zah?

THANK YOU VERY MUCH. THE FOOD IS DELICIOUS.

Molte grazie. Il cibo è ottimo.
MOHL-teh GRAH-tzee-eh. Eel CHEE-boh EH OH-tee-moh.

In the Market

The following phrases will help you make purchases and learn more about unfamiliar produce, spices and herbs.

WHAT ARE THE LOCAL
FRUITS AND VEGETABLES?

Qual è la verdura e la frutta locale?
Kwah-LEH lah vehr-DOO-rah eh lah FROO-tah loh-KAH-leh?

WHAT IS THIS CALLED?

Come si chiama questo?
KOH-meh see kee-AH-mah KWEH-stoh?

DO YOU HAVE . . . HERE?
(ADD AN ITEM FROM THE
FOODS & FLAVORS GUIDE.)

Ha . . . in questo mercato?
Ah . . . een KWEH-stoh mehr-KAH-toh?

MAY I TASTE THIS?

Posso assaggiare questo?
POH-soh ah-sah-JEE-AH-reh KWEH-stoh?

WHERE CAN I BUY
FRESH . . . ?

Dove posso comprare . . . freschi?
*DOH-veh POH-soh kohm-PRAH-reh
. . . FREH-skee?*

HOW MUCH IS THIS PER
KILOGRAM?

Quanto costa questo al chilo?
KWAHN-toh KOH-stah KWEH-stoh ahl KEE-loh?

I WOULD LIKE TO BUY ¼ KILO-
GRAM OF THIS / THAT.

Vorrei comprare un quarto di chilo di questo/quello.
Voh-REH-ee kohm-PRAH-reh oon KWAHR-toh dee KEE-loh dee KWEH-stoh/KWEH-loh.

MAY I PHOTOGRAPH THIS?

Posso fare una fotografia?
POH-soh FAH-reh oo-nah foh-toh-grah-FEE-ah?

Other Useful Phrases

Sometimes it helps to see in writing a word or phrase that is said to you in Italian, because certain letters have distinctly different sounds in Italian than in English. You may be familiar with the word and its English translation but less familiar with its pronunciation. The following phrase comes in handy if you want to see the word or phrase you are hearing.

PLEASE WRITE IT ON MY PIECE OF PAPER.

Per favore me lo scriva su questo pezzo di carta.
Pehr fah-VOH-reh meh loh SKREE-vah soo KWEH-stoh PEH-tzoh dee KAHR-tah.

Interested in bringing home books about Sicilian food?

WHERE CAN I BUY A SICILIAN COOKBOOK IN ENGLISH?

Dove posso comprare un libro di cucina siciliana in inglese?
DOH-veh POH-soh kohm-PRAH-reh oon LEE-broh dee kuh-CHEE-nah see-chee-lee-AH-nah een een-GLEH-seh?

And, of course, the following phrases also are useful to know.

WHERE IS THE LADIES' / MEN'S RESTROOM?

Dov'è il gabinetto per donne/per uomini?
Doh-VEH eel gah-bee-NEH-toh pehr DOH-neh / pehr oo-OH-mee-nee?

MAY I HAVE THE CHECK, PLEASE?

Il conto, per favore?
Eel KOHN-toh, pehr fah-VOH-reh?

DO YOU ACCEPT CREDIT CARDS?

Accetta carte di credito?
Ah-CHEH-tah KAHR-teh dee KREH-dee-toh?

Menu Guide

This alphabetical listing is an extensive compilation of Sicilian menu entries in Italian and in some cases in Sicilian, indicated by (Sic), with English translations to help make ordering food easier. In Italian, *c* and *g* when followed by *e* or *i* have the sound of "ch" and "dg" as in English cherry and jelly, respectively. *Ch* and *gh* have the sound of "k" and "g" as in English chemistry and get. *Gli* is pronounced with a sound English does not have and is similar to "yee." *H* is never aspirated. Besides the above examples with *c* and *g*, it is used in the beginning of a few important words as a way to distinguish homonyms: *ho* (I have) from *o* (or); *ha* (he/she has) from *a* (at); *hanno* (they have) from *anno* (year).

The *Menu Guide* includes typical Sicilian dishes as well as dishes that may only be available locally. Classic local dishes that should not be missed are labeled "local favorite" in the margin next to the menu entry. Some noteworthy dishes popular throughout much of the island—also not to be missed—are labeled "Sicilian classic." Of course, some local favorites are Sicilian favorites as well. Comments on some of our favorites also are included in the margin.

Most Sicilians do not eat breakfast. They drink an espresso coffee before rushing out of the house in the morning, and then have a substantial mid-morning snack in a coffee bar, *pasticceria* (pastry shop) or *rosticceria* (snack shop). But an increasing number of Sicilians begin their day with a very light breakfast (*prima colazione*) around 7 or 8 AM. *Pranzo* is a large meal taken in the late morning or early afternoon. Supper (*cena*) is at 8 or 9 PM, and restaurants typically begin serving at 7:30 or 8 PM. Not surprisingly, Sicilian restaurants range from small neighborhood eateries (*rosticcerie, friggitorie*) to restaurants of various kinds (*pizzerie, trattorie, osterie, ristoranti*) all the way up to upscale establishments in prestigious hotels in urban areas.

We hope you will use this *Menu Guide* in conjunction with the *Foods & Flavors Guide* to explore Sicily's traditional and nouvelle cuisines with confidence. Try to sample as many of these fabulous dishes as you can on your next trip to Sicily!

acciughe marinate anchovies marinated in oil and vinegar.

agnelli pasquali marzipan lambs for Easter. See *pecorelle pasquali,* this *Guide.*

GREAT CHOICE **agnello arrosto** roasted lamb. Lamb typically is cut into pieces and roasted in a pan, but if barbecued over hot coals it is also called *agnello alla brace.*

agnello farcito stuffed lamb.

agnello in fricassea stewed lamb with green peas and onions. When the stew is cooked, raw eggs are scrambled in, and fresh lemon juice is added to the sauce.

alici marinate anchovies marinated in oil and vinegar.

YUMMY **amaretti** almond cookies, made with a mixture of regular and bitter almonds.

ammogghiu (Sic) sauce of olive oil with chopped garlic and parsley, used to moisten and flavor grilled meat or vegetables both during the cooking process and on the plate. With the addition of fresh lemon juice, *ammogghiu* is also used with boiled or grilled fish. In Italian such a sauce is called *salmoriglio.*

SICILIAN CLASSIC **anelletti al forno** baked pasta with a ragout of ground beef and peas, often with pieces of hard-boiled eggs, diced fried eggplant, ham or cheese. This dish requires a typically Sicilian kind of pasta shaped like little rings (*anelletti*), and is featured at nearly every Sunday and holiday family meal in Sicily.

anguille fritte fried eels.

antipasto fritto appetizer of mixed fried foods. Chickpea fritters (*panelle*), potato croquettes and other specialties normally sold in *friggitorie* (fry shops) have become one of the most common antipasti in Sicilian restaurants. Also called *frittura mista.*

SICILIAN CLASSIC **arancine** "little oranges." Deep-fried, saffron-colored rice balls, so named because of their round shape and golden color. *Arancine* may be round or cone-shaped.

arancine agli spinaci *arancine* filled with spinach and béchamel sauce. *See arancine.*

arancine al burro *arancine* filled with ham, mozzarella cheese and béchamel sauce. See *arancine.*

arancine alla carne *arancine* filled with a ragout of ground beef and peas, and possibly pine nuts and currants. See *arancine.*

aricciola o ricciola alla ghiotta amberjack stew with tomatoes, capers and olives.

aricciola o ricciola all'acqua di mare amberjack cooked in seawater. Also called *aricciola all'acqua pazza.*

GOOD CHOICE **aricciola o ricciola arrosto** grilled amberjack.

arista di maiale al pistacchio roast pork loin with pistachios.

arrosto misto mixed grilled meats.

arrosto panato alla palermitana Palermo-style grilled, breaded beef. Also called *bistecca panata.*

babbaluci (Sic) con aglio e prezzemelo small land snails cooked with olive oil, garlic and parsley. In a tradition that was more common in the past, they are sold on the streets of the old part of Palermo for the feast of the patron saint Rosalia.

baccalà al forno baked salted cod, usually accompanied by potatoes. To eliminate the salt, the fish is soaked in water for a few days and some milk is added to the pan during baking.

baccalà fritto deep-fried salted cod. To remove the salt, the fish is soaked in water for a few days prior to cooking.

baci panteschi crunchy layers of fried dough shaped like a flower or butterfly and filled with sweet ricotta cheese. The name means "Pantelleria-style kisses" to distinguish them from the famous *baci* chocolate candy kisses known throughout Italy.

biancomangiare blancmange sauce or pudding made with milk, sugar and cornstarch, which is the basis for many Sicilian sweets. Also called *crema di latte.*

biscotti con il vino cookies made with white wine in the dough. These cookies, typical of Aidone in the province of Enna, have an unusual shape meant to represent an Easter dove.

biscotti di San Martino round, dry, very hard cookies eaten for the feast of Saint Martin (November 11th). They may be elaborately decorated with sugar icing. Plain *biscotti di San Martino* are not very sweet and are normally dipped in sweet wine (*Marsala, moscato* or *passito*) to soften them for eating.

biscotti regina "queens' biscuits," cookies sold in most bakeries in Palermo, and also available in Erice and other towns. They are covered with sesame seeds. Also called *reginelle.*

bistecca panata Palermo-style grilled, breaded meat. Also called *arrosto panato alla palermitana.*

bollito boiled meat. A stock is obtained from a large cut of meat boiled with carrots, celery, onions, potatoes and a few tomatoes. The meat is then cut in thick slices. It can be served cold, dressed with olive oil and fresh lemon juice or with *salsa verde.* It is also served warm, with the boiled vegetables and *patate allo zafferano* (saffron potatoes). The stock may be used to cook risotto, tortellini or other small kinds of pasta.

SICILIAN CLASSIC   **braciolone** braised, stuffed meat roll, cooked in tomato sauce. See *falsomagro*.

SICILIAN CLASSIC   **brioche con gelato** sweet bun cut open and filled with *gelato*, with an optional topping of whipped cream. The freshness of the bun is crucial to the success of this messy but delicious treat.

broccoli (Sic) all'agrigentina Agrigento-style cauliflower with *caciocavallo* cheese and whole black olives. Also called *cavolfiori all'agrigentina*.

GREAT   **broccoli (Sic) in pastella** cauliflower dipped in a thick, yeasty batter, and then deep-fried. See *verdure in pastella*. Also called *cavolfiori in pastella*.

bruschetta toasted bread with chopped raw tomatoes.

SICILIAN CLASSIC   **buccellato** Christmas ring cake filled with mixed chopped nuts and dried figs. *Buccellati* can vary in size, shape, and filling in different parts of the island. For example, small ones (*buccellatini*) are not always round, and in Castelbuono small *buccellati* are called *cosi chini* ("filled things" in Sicilian). The small, round version is called *cuddureddi* in Sicilian. In Caltagirone *buccellatini* come in four flavors: pistachio, almond, cooked wine and honey. In Piana degli Albanesi, a town near Palermo, there is a type of *buccellato* filled with an almond and white-melon preserve. *Buccellato* is called *cucciddatu* in Sicilian.

SICILIAN CLASSIC   **caciocavallo (cacio) all'argentiera** "silversmith's cheese." Slices of fresh *caciocavallo* cheese are lightly cooked with vinegar, oregano and sugar. This dish is one of many "poor" dishes intended to give oneself and envious neighbors (including a mysterious silversmith's wife) the illusion of eating the foods of the rich. Also called *formaggio all'argentiera*.

calamari arrosto grilled squid. Also called *calamari alla brace* if cooked over hot coals.

GOOD CHOICE   **calamari fritti** deep-fried squid.

calamari in umido stew of squid with tomatoes, olive oil, and garlic. Also called *calamari in tegame* ("in the pot") or *calamari in guazzetto* ("splashing").

calamari ripieni squid stuffed with a mixture of toasted bread crumbs, pine nuts and currants. On the island of Pantelleria, almonds and capers are added to the stuffing.

caldarroste roasted chestnuts. See *castagne abbrustolite*.

VERY GOOD   **calzone al forno** baked turnover made from pizza dough stuffed with mozzarella and ham. It is baked in the wood ovens of pizzerias normally open only in the evening. A smaller version, either baked or fried (*calzone fritto*), is sold as a snack in *rosticcerie* or coffee bars, especially early in the day.

cannoli Sicilian dessert, originally typical of Carnival, but now available year-round. The dough, which includes cinnamon, Marsala wine and lard, is wrapped around a tube (*cannolo*), fried, and filled with sweet ricotta cream. Connoiseurs have their *cannoli* filled on the spot (*espressi*) because the crust can quickly become soggy. Small *cannoli* are called *cannolicchi* (Sic). **SICILIAN CLASSIC**

caponata sweet-and-sour eggplant dish, served cold or at room temperature. It requires an accurate balance of ingredients (tomatoes, onions, capers, celery and olives), and originally may have included a kind of fish called *capone* (hence the name *caponata*). Messina has a type of *caponata* that includes dried cod (*stoccafisso alla messinese*), and on the island of Pantelleria some restaurants make it with shrimp, swordfish, bitter cocoa and salted, pressed roe (*bottarga*). **SICILIAN CLASSIC**

cappidduzzi (Sic) fritti fried ravioli filled with cinnamon-flavored sweet sheep's milk ricotta cream and small candied lemon rinds. This dish, which is very similar to *cassatelle di ricotta,* is typical of the town of Marsala.

cappuccetti fritti fried baby squid. *Cappuccetti* ("little hoods") describes their shape. Also called *seppioline fritte.*

capretto arrosto roasted kid. Baby goat barbecued over hot coals (*alla brace*) or, more often, cut into pieces and baked in a pan. It is a typical main dish served on Easter Sunday. **GREAT CHOICE**

capuliato (Sic) di pomodoro sauce made from sun-dried tomatoes.

carciofata sweet-and-sour dish similar to *caponata,* but with artichokes in place of eggplant. See *caponata,* this *Guide.*

carciofi al ragù artichokes stuffed with an egg mixture and cooked in tomato sauce.

carciofi alla giudìa Jewish-style artichokes. Elsewhere in Italy, particularly in Rome, *carciofi alla giudìa* are blanched, deep-fried artichokes. But in Sicily the dish is quite different. In one of its many versions, artichokes are filled with a mixture of toasted bread crumbs, pine nuts and currants, then cooked in a saucepan.

carciofi alla villanella peasant-style artichokes, chopped and cooked in a saucepan with olive oil and garlic.

carciofi arrostiti roasted artichokes. A mixture of olive oil, chopped mint and garlic is poured into artichoke hearts, which are then wrapped in aluminium foil and roasted over hot coals or in warm ashes. Also called *carciofi alla brace.* **GREAT**

carciofi fritti in pastella artichokes dipped in a thick, yeasty batter, then deep-fried.

carciofi ripieni stuffed artichokes. Depending on the stuffing, they may be similar to *carciofi alla giudìa* or *carciofi al ragù*.

carciofini sott'olio pickled baby artichokes in olive oil.

cardi in pastella celery-like stalks of the domesticated thistle (cardoon) dipped in a thick, yeasty batter and then deep-fried.

carne a sfincione sliced veal or beef cooked in a pan with potatoes and onions, tomatoes, bread crumbs, cheese and oregano, ingredients that top *sfincione*. See *sfincione*, this *Guide*.

carne aglassata (Sic) glazed pot roast. It is prepared with a cut of young steer meat. The gravy (*glassa*) from this dish may be used to dress pasta.

WONDERFUL **carpaccio di pesce spada** thinly sliced raw swordfish, dressed with olive oil and fresh lemon juice.

carpaccio di tonno thinly sliced raw tuna, dressed with olive oil and fresh lemon juice.

LOCAL FAVORITE **cartocciate** baked, stuffed turnover similar to *calzone al forno,* but made with a sweeter brioche dough rather than pizza dough. It is typical of Catania.

SICILIAN CLASSIC **cassata** classic Sicilian cake of Arabic origin. It is assembled from layers of sponge cake and almond paste (marzipan), which line the sides of a pan. The pan is then filled with sweet ricotta cream. The cake is turned upside down and beautifully decorated with icing, candied fruit and zucchini preserves. Traditionally an Easter cake, *cassata* is now available year-round.

SICILIAN CLASSIC **cassata al forno** baked *cassata* in which a pastry crust substitutes for the sponge cake and almond paste. This less elaborated and less sweet version of the *cassata* is often homemade. See *cassata.*

LOCAL FAVORITE **cassatelle di Agira** sweet fried turnovers filled with chickpea and almond flour. They are a specialty of Agira in the province of Enna.

cassatelle di ceci sweet fried turnovers filled with puréed chickpeas, prepared in some towns for St. Joseph's celebrations (March 19th).

LOCAL FAVORITE **cassatelle di ricotta** fried turnovers filled with sweet ricotta cream, a famous specialty of the province of Trapani. They are incredibly delicious, especially when still warm.

castagne abbrustolite chestnuts roasted in portable coal stoves and sold in the streets in the fall. Also called *caldarroste.*

castagne secche shelled, dried chestnuts sold in the streets.

SICILIAN CLASSIC **castrato arrosto** meat from a castrated sheep (believed to be more tender) roasted or grilled on hot coals (*alla brace*). *Castrato* is the most typical barbecue meat in Sicily, especially for holiday outings.

cavolfiori all'agrigentina cauliflower, Agrigento-style, with *caciocavallo* cheese and whole black olives. Also called *broccoli all'agrigentina.*

cavolfiori in pastella cauliflower dipped in a thick, yeasty batter and then deep-fried. Also called *broccoli in pastella.* SICILIAN CLASSIC

cedrata citron preserves, used as a filling in cakes.

cernia alla marinara grouper stewed in a small quantity of tomato sauce. Also called *cernia in umido.*

cernia marinata marinated grouper. A typical marinade consists of olive oil and fresh lemon juice, with the possible addition of bay leaves, black pepper and mint leaves.

cervello fritto fried beef brains.

chiacchere strips of fried dough, sprinkled with powdered sugar. *Chiacchere* ("gossips") are sold in most bakeries at Carnival time. They originated in northern Italy but have gained popularity in Sicily.

ciakiciuka (Sic) Pantellerian dish of stewed vegetables.

ciambella ring-shaped cake.

cicirelli fritti fried *cicirelli,* long, thin fish similar to smelt.

cioccolata di Modica traditional chocolate from the town of Modica. LOCAL FAVORITE

cipollata di sgombro boiled mackerel, served cold with vinegar and a large quantity of onions browned in olive oil.

cipollata di tonno fresh boiled tuna, served cold and dressed with vinegar, capers and plenty of onions that have been browned in olive oil. Also called *tonno con cipolle.*

coniglio alla cacciatora braised rabbit, hunter's-style, with a sauce of tomatoes, sometimes with mushrooms.

coniglio alla portuìsa rabbit made with potatoes, carrots, onions, olives, sweet peppers and capers. The dish is typical of Chiaramonte Gulfi in the province of Ragusa.

coniglio alla stemperata rabbit marinated in wine, dredged in flour, fried in olive oil and then cooked lightly in vinegar.

coniglio in agrodolce sweet-and-sour rabbit. It is similar to *coniglio alla stemperata,* but a bit sweeter.

coniglio ripieno al forno baked stuffed rabbit.

cornetti croissants. Cornetti means "little horns," which describes their shape. Traditionally they are filled with jam or custard, although newer fillings such as hazelnut cream and almonds are becoming popular.

cosi chini (Sic) name for *buccellatini* (small Christmas ring cakes) that is used in Castelbuono. See *buccellato.*

LOCAL FAVORITE **costata di maiale ripiena** stuffed pork chops, especially famous in Chiaramonte Gulfi, the town where "pork is king," and where the stuffing includes salami and hard-boiled egg. In the province of Agrigento *costata di maiale ripiena* typically is incised with garlic and pecorino cheese. Also called *cuoste chini* (Sic), "full ribs."

GOOD CHOICE **costolette di agnello arrosto** grilled lamb chops. If cooked over hot coals, they may be called *costolette di agnello alla brace*.

costolette di maiale arrosto grilled pork chops. If cooked over hot coals, they may be called *costolette di maiale alla brace*.

YUMMY **cotognata** quince paste. This autumn treat traditionally was made in decorative ceramic molds.

WONDERFUL **cozze al gratin** mussels au gratin. Mussels broiled on the half shell with toasted bread crumbs, currants and pine nuts.

cozze scoppiate "burst mussels." Mussels cooked in a covered pot until they open, then served with plenty of black pepper as the only dressing. Also called *impepata di cozze*. The dish is a simpler version of *zuppa di cozze*.

crema di latte blancmange. See *biancomangiare,* this *Guide*.

cremolata di mandorla almond ice. Similar to *granita di mandorla*.

LOCAL FAVORITE **crespelle** fritters filled with fresh ricotta cheese or anchovy fillets. They are typical of the Catania province. See *sfinci*.

crocchè di latte milk croquettes, with very thick béchamel sauce mixed with egg yolks substituting for potatoes.

GREAT **crocchè di patate** potato croquettes, popularly called *cazzilli* ("little pricks").

crostata di mandorle almond tart.

crostata di mele Sicilian apple tart. Personal-size tarts are *crostatine*.

YUMMY **cubbaita (Sic)** sesame seed confection, similar to brittle. A boiling paste of sesame seeds, mixed nuts, honey and sugar is flattened on a marble surface and, when partially cooled, cut into diamond-shaped pieces. Also called *giuggiolena,* an Italian word for sesame seeds. In Caltagirone in the province of Catania you may find a type of *cubbaita* made with chickpeas instead of sesame seeds.

LOCAL FAVORITE **cuccìa (Sic)** pudding prepared with whole wheat berries for St. Lucy's day (December 13th), when many Sicilians traditionally do not eat anything made with flour.

cucciddatu (Sic) Christmas ring cake. See *buccellato*.

cucunci (Sic) sott'olio caper berries (the fruit of the caper plant), pickled and packed in olive oil. *Cucunci* can also be purchased *sott'aceto* (packed in vinegar), *sotto sale* (in sea salt) or *al naturale* (as they are).

cuddrireddre (Sic) traditional Carnival sweet from Delia in the province of Caltanissetta. Cinnamon-flavored dough is thinly rolled, elaborately twisted and fried. A special recognition from the Slow Food International Movement has saved *cuddrireddre* from disappearance.

cuddura cull'ova (Sic) a round cake with unshelled hard-boiled eggs baked inside. It is an Easter specialty in Catania.

cuddureddi (Sic) small, round version of the Christmas cake called *cucciddatu* (SIC) or *buccellato*. See *buccellato*.

cudduruni (Sic) type of pizza typical of Agrigento, but also common in central and eastern Sicily. It is similar to a *calzone*.

cuoste chini (Sic) stuffed pork chops. See *costata di maiale ripiena*.

cuscus di pesce couscous with fish. In Trapani province, the couscous is served with a rather liquid fish and tomato sauce. On the small island of Pantelleria, it is served with sauce, vegetables (zucchini, eggplant, peppers) and an entire fish.

cuscus dolce a sweet couscous dish. The couscous is usually mixed with sweet ricotta cheese, flavored with cinnamon, and sprinkled with chocolate and pistachios.

dentice arrosto grilled sea bream.

dolci alla carruba carob pastries typical of Modica and also made in Palazzolo Acreide, both in the province of Ragusa.

ericini small cakes filled with citron preserves, typical of the town of Erice.

falsomagro braised meat roll. A large, thick slice of beef is cut nearly in half, opened like a book, covered with a layer of mortadella and rolled around a mixture of ingredients with whole hard-boiled eggs inside. The stuffed meat roll is then braised. Versions with a stuffing of ground beef are also known. *Falsomagro* and *braciolone* often are used synonymously, although local preparations may distinguish between them.

fave a coniglio fava beans boiled and dressed with olive oil, garlic and (optionally) vinegar. *A coniglio* means rabbit-style, perhaps because rabbit used to be dressed in the same way. Also called *fave lesse* or *fave bollite*. The beans used for this dish are fresh, but large enough to have a tough outer skin, which people avoid by squeezing the soft beans into their mouths individually.

fegatini di pollo con patate chicken livers stewed with potatoes.

fegato ai Sette Cannoli sweet-and-sour preparation of winter squash with orange flesh. Sette Cannoli ("Seven Pipes") is a poor Palermitan neighborhood that used to have a fountain with seven spouts. This "meaty" squash dish may have been the closest that most residents of this poor neighborhood normally got to meat, and so it was dubbed "Seven Pipes' liver," *fegato ai Sette Cannoli.* Also called *zucca all'agrodolce.*

filetto di suino (maiale) nero dei Nebrodi al Nero d'Avola fillet of black pig braised in Nero d'Avola, an increasingly popular wine. Black pigs native to the Nebrodi Mountains of Sicily are highly prized for their delicious meat.

LOCAL FAVORITE **filletta** soft, round sponge cake, often with a sprinkling of local pistachios. It is a specialty of Bronte.

finocchietto selvatico panato wild fennel stalks, breaded with toasted bread crumbs and fried.

focaccia con gli spinaci crunchy spinach pizza. See *fuazza con gli spinaci,* this *Guide.*

WONDERFUL **formaggio alla piastra** grilled cheese. Slightly seasoned cheeses are particularly suitable for this dish. Some favorites are *primosale, caciocavallo,* and less frequently, *fiore sicano* and *piacentino.* Also called *formaggio grigliato.*

formaggio all'argentiera "silversmith's cheese." See *caciocavallo (cacio) all'argentiera,* this *Guide.*

frascatole (Sic) in brodo di pesce e gamberi larger pieces of handmade couscous called *frascatole,* served with a broth of fish and shrimp. It is typical of the province of Trapani. See *cuscus di pesce.*

frittata di asparagi omelet with tender wild asparagus shoots or cultivated asparagus. It may include ricotta cheese.

frittata di fiori di zucca zucchini-blossom omelet.

frittata di gamberi shrimp omelet.

GOOD CHOICE **frittata di verdure** omelet with vegetables. A seemingly infinite number of variations on this omelet are possible, using different vegetables or wild herbs in various combinations.

frittella spring vegetable medley with fresh peas, fava beans and artichokes. The tender young vegetables are steamed, sprinkled with vinegar and served cold.

VERY GOOD **fritto misto (di pesce)** mixed fried seafood, usually including shrimp and squid.

frittola (Sic) a street food of refried butcher scraps (*ciccioli*) made from rendered fat, sold in historical markets in Palermo.

Because *frittola* is very spicy and most of its lovers like to enjoy it with wine, it is often sold just outside an *osteria,* a shop where inexpensive unbottled wine is sold. The piping-hot *frittola* is sold from hand-woven baskets, covered with a kitchen cloth.

frittura mista appetizer of mixed fried foods. See *antipasto fritto.*   WONDERFUL

fuazza (Sic) con gli spinaci crunchy rolled pizza with spinach, similar to *impignolata.* It is typical of the province of Agrigento. Fuazza is the Sicilian word for *focaccia;* the dish is also called *focaccia con gli spinaci.*

funciddi (Sic) dry cookies made with almonds and hazelnuts, a Christmas specialty of Buccheri in the province of Syracuse.

funghi arrosto grilled mushrooms.

funghi sott'olio pickled mushrooms packed in olive oil.

funghi trifolati stir-fried mushrooms with olive oil, garlic and parsley.

gamberoni arrosto grilled giant prawns. One of the best (and most   GREAT CHOICE
expensive) entries on the Sicilian menu!

gattò (Sic) di patate potato dish similar to American shepherd's pie, usually eaten for supper at home. Potatoes are boiled, peeled, mashed and mixed with grated Parmesan cheese and eggs. Either ground beef and green peas or béchamel sauce, cheese and ham are placed between two layers of the potato mixture, and the whole thing is then broiled in the oven. Browned bread crumbs on top make it look like a cake, hence the name *gattò* (from French *gateau,* "cake").

gelato milk-based ice cream traditionally made without eggs or   GREAT
milk fat.

gelo di mellone watermelon pudding believed to be of Arabic   SICILIAN CLASSIC
origin, decorated with chopped pistachios, chocolate shavings and sometimes jasmine flowers.

gemelle a round, dry cookie with thin, white icing found in Aidone in the province of Enna. See *savoiardi,* this *Guide.*

genovesi small cakes filled with custardy pastry cream (*crema*   LOCAL FAVORITE
pasticcera or *crema gialla*) or sweet ricotta cheese. *Genovesi* are particularly famous in Erice. True connoisseurs of *genovesi* wait for warm ones, just taken out of the oven (*genovesi calde*). See *Recipes,* p. 68.

giri (Sic) bolliti boiled Swiss chard, usually dressed with olive oil and fresh lemon juice.

gisieri (Sic) di pollo chicken gizzards cooked in a pot, often with chicken livers.

giuggiolena sesame seed confection, similar to brittle. See *cubbaita*.

granita di caffè coffee ice. Other popular flavors are mulberry (*granita di gelso*), lemon (*granita di limone*) and almond (*granita di mandorla*), which is similar to *cremolata di mandorla*.

impanata (Sic) small pie or turnover stuffed with meat, cheese, or vegetable fillings. *Impanate* are typical of eastern Sicily.

LOCAL FAVORITE **impanatigghi (Sic)** small cakes with an unusual ground beef and chocolate filling. They are a specialty of the town of Modica.

impepata di cozze mussels with black pepper. See *cozze scoppiate.*

impignolata (Sic) type of pizza typical of Porto Empedocle in the province of Agrigento.

inciminateddi (Sic) Sicilian name for *panini inciminati,* small loaves of bread totally covered with sesame seeds.

infigghiulata (Sic) di ricotta traditional pizza filled with tomato, onions, sliced dry sausage and ricotta cheese. It is typical of some towns in central and eastern Sicily, especially in the Enna and Ragusa provinces. *Infigghiulata* is folded four times. Each layer is topped with the same ingredients, and in the end it acquires a rectangular shape.

infriulata (Sic) stuffed pizza that is a Christmas tradition in Ciminna in the province of Palermo.

SICILIAN CLASSIC **insalata di arance** orange salad. Oranges are peeled, sliced, mixed with smoked herring and sliced scallions, and dressed with olive oil and salt. The oranges used are the rather acid and sharp-flavored Portualli variety (Sicilian for Portuguese).

VERY GOOD **insalata di finocchi** salad made with cultivated (not wild) fennel.

SICILIAN CLASSIC **insalata di mare** sea salad of boiled octopus chunks mixed with chopped parsley, diced carrots and celery, and dressed with olive oil. Served cold or at room temperature.

insalata di pomodori tomato salad, dressed with olive oil, oregano, and salt.

LOCAL FAVORITE **insalata di stocco** dried-cod salad, typical of the province of Messina. Also called *insalata di stoccafisso.*

insalata mista mixed salad of lettuce and tomatoes.

insalata palermitana salad with tomatoes, red onions from Tropea (Calabria), boiled string beans and chopped potatoes, all dressed with olive oil, oregano and salt. It is a common home food in Palermo.

insalata russa Russian salad, a mixture of diced boiled vegetables and fish, dressed with mayonnaise, served cold or at room temperature. Although this is not a Sicilian dish, it is often served as an appetizer or side dish with elegant dinners.

involtini alla siciliana Sicilian skewered meat rolls. Thin slices of veal or beef are rolled around a mixture of toasted bread crumbs, pine nuts, currants and cheese, skewered three or four at a time with slices of onion and bay leaves and grilled. Also called *spiedini alla siciliana*. See *Recipes,* p. 59. — SICILIAN CLASSIC

involtini di melanzane eggplant rolls. Slices of eggplant are grilled or fried and then rolled around a mixture of toasted bread crumbs, pine nuts, currants and cheese. — SICILIAN CLASSIC

involtini di pesce spada swordfish rolls. They may be filled with currants and pine nuts or with olives, capers and toasted bread crumbs. It is a traditional dish of Messina. — LOCAL FAVORITE

involtini di spatola scabbard fish rolls. They are a cheaper version of swordfish rolls. See *involtini di pesce spada.*

latte di mandorla almond milk. A favorite cold summer drink made from sugar and ground almonds. In Erice the mixture is available for sale, ready to be diluted in water and chilled.

lingua di vitello marinata marinated veal tongue.

lingua di vitello lessa boiled veal tongue.

lingue di suocera "mother-in-law's tongues," an apt name for these long, curved, chocolate-covered cookies!

lumache a picchio pacchio (Sic) land snails cooked in a pot with olive oil, garlic, parsley and a few tomatoes. *Babbaluci* (Sic), the smallest land snails, are not usually cooked in this style.

maccu (macco) (Sic) thick soup made from dried fava beans. It is flavored with wild fennel sprigs and dressed with olive oil. It may have pasta cooked in it. See *Recipes,* p. 46. — SICILIAN CLASSIC

macedonia di frutta fresca fresh fruit cocktail. Maraschino liqueur is often added.

maiale alla chiaramontana pork stewed in the pot in the style of Chiaramonte Gulfi in the province of Ragusa.

maiale nero al forno baked black pig. Black pigs native to the Nebrodi Mountains are highly prized for their delicious meat.

maiolini in umido baby octopus stew. See *polipetti in umido. Maiolini* have two rows of suckers on their arms.

masculini (Sic) fritti fried anchovies, which are called *masculini* in the Catania area. — LOCAL FAVORITE

melanzane a cotoletta breaded, fried eggplant.

melanzane a quaglia eggplant cut to look like the tail of a quail, and then deep-fried. The dish is a fry-shop favorite in Palermo.

GREAT **melanzane alla parmigiana** eggplant Parmesan. Fried egglant slices are layered with tomato sauce and plenty of grated Parmesan cheese. Sliced cheese and ham may be included.

melanzane ammuttunate (Sic) stuffed eggplants. Whole baby eggplants are incised with cloves of garlic, mint and pecorino cheese, then browned in olive oil and stewed in tomato sauce.

GOOD CHOICE **melanzane arrostite** roasted eggplant. Slices of eggplant are grilled, preferably over hot coals, and then dressed in olive oil, garlic and parsley.

melanzane sott'olio pickled eggplant packed in olive oil with garlic.

millefoglie "one thousand layers," sweet buns sold in bakeries. Versions made of rolled pasta dough or puff pastry and filled with custard and fruit are sold in pastry shops.

GOOD CHOICE **minestra di ceci** chickpea soup. Pasta, usually *ditalini* ("little thimbles"), may be cooked in it.

SICILIAN CLASSIC **minestra di fagioli freschi** fresh bean soup. Fresh beans are available in Sicily in the summer. They are shelled and boiled with onions and a few tomatoes. *Spaghetti tagliati* ("spaghetti broken into small pieces") are cooked in this liquid to create the dish. In the summer this soup may be served cold. Also called *minestra di fagioli incirati* (Sic) and (in Catania) *triaca a'pasta* (Sic).

GOOD CHOICE **minestra di fave** thick soup made from dried fava beans. It is similar to *maccu* (this *Guide*), but thicker. If water is added to the beans, pasta may be cooked in it. In Modica a special kind of pasta called *lolli* is used; see *Foods & Flavors Guide*.

minne (Sic) di vergini "virgin's breasts." Cakes shaped like women's breasts and filled with blancmange and bits of zucchini preserves called *zuccata*. Once made by the nuns in several convents in Sicily, they can still be found in a pastry shop in Sambuca in the province of Agrigento. St. Agatha protects the breasts and is always portrayed carrying a plate with breasts on it. St. Agatha is the patron saint of Catania, where these pastries are called *minne di Sant'Agata* ("St. Agatha's breasts"). In Catania they are filled with sweet ricotta cream, covered with green almond paste and a layer of white icing, then topped with a cherry. They are especially visible around the time of St. Agatha's feast (February 5th).

moscardini in umido baby octopus stew. See *polipetti in umido*. *Moscardini* have only one row of suckers on their arms.

mostaccioli wide variety of hard biscuits. Historically the biscuits were sweetened with *vino cotto,* concentrated from *mosto* (must; grape juice). In many parts of Sicily, they still are. But in Palermo today, *mostaccioli* today contain no *vino cotto.* White sugar is used as the sweetener and the biscuits puff up during baking. Erice's *mostaccioli* are long and hard with a criss-cross pattern formerly made with a special tool called a *pettine* ("comb"), but today made using a wooden mold. These biscuits, flavored with cinnamon and cloves, are meant to be softened in sweet wine. SICILIAN CLASSIC

mussu (Sic) boiled lamb's snout, cheeks, nerves and cartilage; sold in historical markets.

napoli sweets with layers of lemon- and cinnamon-flavored marzipan and icing that is half chocolate and half vanilla. They are a specialty of Enna, where they were made by the nuns of St. Mark's convent.

nucatoli (Sic) wide variety of rather hard cookies, often sweetened with honey. Several kinds of *nucatoli* are also called *mostaccioli.* See *mostaccioli,* this *Guide.*

olive al forno baked black olives.

olive cunzati (Sic) green olives dressed in olive oil, garlic and oregano. Diced carrots and celery may be included. EXCELLENT

olivette di Sant'Agata marzipan olives created especially for the Feast of St. Agatha in Catania.

orata arrosto grilled gilthead fish. GOOD CHOICE

ossa di morti "bones of the dead," cookies shaped like shinbones, traditionally available for the feast of All Souls' Day (November 2nd) or Christmas.

pan di Spagna sponge cake.

pane con la milza bun filled with a mixture of liver, lungs and spleen (*milza*), from which the sandwich takes its name. It may be served alone (*schietta* (Sic), "unmarried") or with fresh ricotta and grated *caciocavallo* cheese (*maritata* (Sic),"married"). Special shops in Palermo cater to the many aficionados of this unique specialty. Also called *pani ca meusa* in Sicilian. LOCAL FAVORITE

LOCAL FAVORITE   **pane e panelle** bun stuffed with a piping hot, salted chickpea fritter (see *panelle,* this *Guide*). Once the traditional lunch of laborers, *pane e panelle* is now a celebrated street food and the passion of Palermitans, including students, who eat it as a mid-morning snack.

GREAT   **pane nero di Castelvetrano** black bread from Castelvetrano in the province of Trapani. This bread has earned special recognition from the Slow Food International Movement.

pane rimacinato classic Sicilian bread made from *rimacinato,* twice-milled, hard durum wheat flour. It has a hard brown crust, and a golden color inside. It is the most common kind of bread in smaller towns, where it is often baked in brick ovens.

LOCAL FAVORITE   **panelle** chickpea fritters, sold in fry shops in Palermo. Chickpea flour is mixed with water, spread on a marble slab, cut into rectangles, and deep-fried.

pani ca meusa (Sic) bun filled with a mixture of liver, lungs and spleen. See *pane con la milza.*

panini inciminati (Sic) small loaves of bread totally covered with sesame seeds. Also called *inciminateddi* in Sicilian. Most Sicilian bread has at least a sprinkle of sesame seeds, a custom believed to be of Arabic origin.

pantofole small cakes from Lercara Friddi in the province of Palermo. They are made with a pastry dough filled with almonds and zucchini preserves, and called *pantofole* ("slippers") because of their shape.

parfait di mandorle almond ice cream. See *semifreddo alle mandorle.*

passavulanti (Sic) almond cookies with glazing.

pasta a picchio pacchio (Sic) pasta dressed with a sauce made from peeled, chopped tomatoes (including seeds) cooked with garlic and olive oil.

SICILIAN CLASSIC   **pasta aglio olio peperoncino** pasta dressed with olive oil, garlic and red pepper. Also called *pasta alla carrettiera.*

pasta ai quattro formaggi pasta dressed with four cheeses.

pasta alla carrettiera pasta dressed with olive oil, garlic and red pepper. This dish is called "cart driver's pasta" because, thanks to its simplicity, it would have been well-suited to a cart driver's hard life. Also called *pasta aglio olio peperoncino.*

pasta alla cucunciata (Sic) pasta dressed with *cucunci,* the fruit of the caper plant. See *cucunci, Foods & Flavors Guide.*

SICILIAN CLASSIC   **pasta alla Norma** pasta with tomato sauce, diced fried eggplant and grated salted ricotta. (Salted ricotta is hard and can be grated.) According to legend, Catanese composer Vincenzo Bellini suggested the name of the dish to the chef of a restaurant near the opera house where he was rehearsing his famous opera, "Norma."

pasta con acciughe e mollica (Sic) pasta with toasted bread crumbs and anchovy fillets. Anchovies are dissolved in olive oil together with a small quantity of sun-dried tomato extract (see *estratto di pomodoro, Foods & Flavors Guide*). SICILIAN CLASSIC

pasta con gamberi e zucchine pasta with shrimp and zucchini. For this dish, which has become a classic, fresh pasta such as *trofie* (see *Foods & Flavors Guide*) is often used. Zucchini blossoms can also be used instead of or together with zucchini. GOOD CHOICE

pasta con i broccoli arriminati (Sic) pasta stir-fried with a cauliflower sauce with currants, pine nuts, saffron and anchovies dissolved in olive oil. *Bucatini,* long spaghetti with a hole (*buco*) inside, is the best pasta to use for this dish. Also called *pasta con i broccoli in tegame*. SICILIAN CLASSIC

pasta con il pomodoro crudo pasta dressed with a marinade of diced, fresh tomatoes, garlic and basil leaves.

pasta con le fave pasta with fava beans. Depending on the season, it may be made with tender, fresh fava beans, often with the addition of fresh ricotta cheese, or with dried fava beans soaked overnight, in which case a small kind of pasta is used.

pasta con le sarde saffron-colored pasta with fresh sardines, wild fennel leaves and a small dollop of sun-dried tomato extract (see *estratto di pomodoro, Foods & Flavors Guide*). This famous Palermitan dish is considered by many to be the Sicilian "national" dish. It is traditionally prepared with pasta such as *bucatini* thick enough to have a hole (*buco*) inside. Legend has it that *pasta con le sarde* was created by the Arabs when they arrived in Mazara in the 800s. In towns far from the sea, particularly in the Madonie Mountains, where sardines are hard to come by, the same dressing is prepared without fish, and called *con le sarde a mare* ("with sardines in the sea"). Agrigento has a version of *pasta con le sarde* that includes regular tomato sauce. This pasta would not be dressed with grated cheese, but may be topped with toasted bread crumbs. SICILIAN CLASSIC

pasta con melanzane pasta with tomato sauce and diced fried eggplant. Also see *pasta alla Norma*.

pasta con pesce spada pasta dressed with a tomato sauce with diced swordfish and chopped mint. Fried diced eggplant, zucchini or mozzarella cheese may be added to the sauce. Flat pastas such as fettuccine or linguine are typically used for this dish, and the sauce often is made with a well-known type of cherry tomato cultivated near Pachino in the province of Syracuse. GOOD CHOICE pasta con salsiccia di cinghiale pasta with wild boar sausage.

pasta con salsiccia e ricotta pasta with sausage and ricotta cheese.

pasta con sugo di cinghiale pasta with wild boar sauce.

SICILIAN CLASSIC pasta con tenerumi (Sic) pasta with zucchini (*zucchina lunga*) leaves and peeled tomatoes cooked in olive oil and garlic.

pasta con zucchini fritti pasta with thinly sliced zucchini fried in olive oil. The frying oil may then be added to the pasta.

pasta di San Giuseppe pasta dressed for the feast of St. Joseph (March 19th). The dish varies greatly in different parts of Sicily. In certain neighborhoods of Palermo, all the leftovers in the pantry, especially beans, are used in the dressing. In Santa Croce di Camerina in the province of Ragusa, many spices are added to a tomato sauce. In Salemi, a town in the province of Trapani famous for beautiful St. Joseph's bread altars, pasta is dressed with toasted bread crumbs and honey or sugar!

pasta incaciata (Sic) pasta layered with slices of eggplant and plenty of cheese, then baked.

pasta reale di Mistretta sweets with a round pastry crust (*pasta frolla*) base and beautiful hand-molded white marzipan (*pasta reale*) shapes on top, a specialty of Mistretta in the province of Messina. Mistretta marzipan is very soft and delicate, in shapes that resemble baroque sculptures.

patate a sfincione *sfincione*-style potatoes, baked with onions, tomatoes, bread crumbs, cheese and oregano. It is a meatless version of *carne a sfincione*.

patate al forno roasted potatoes. The potatoes are peeled, diced and baked in the same pan as the meal's meat (especially kid or lamb). They are usually flavored with rosemary.

patate allo zafferano saffron-colored potatoes. They are cooked with saffron or with a cheaper coloring agent.

paté di olive olive pâté. Though not an original Sicilian product, pâtés have become popular on the island.

SICILIAN CLASSIC pecorelle pasquali Easter lambs made of marzipan (see *pasta reale, Foods & Flavors Guide*). This traditional Easter sweet represents Jesus Christ as a sacrificial lamb. It is decorated with ribbons and a red paper flag representing Resurrection. Favara in the province of Agrigento is famous for making *pecorelle* with a pistachio filling. Erice's *pecorelle* have a unique style. They are flat rather than three-dimensional, and they are filled with citron preserve. Each one is shaped by hand, not molded. The hoofs and wool curls are patiently carved one by one, and a delightful pink tongue is clearly visible in their mouths. *Pecorelle pasquali* also are called *agnelli pasquali*.

TOP LEFT A garden medley of Sicily's fresh fruits and vegetables. **TOP RIGHT** Artful presentation of *antipasti misti,* assorted appetizers, at Trattoria il Maestro del Brodo, Palermo. **MIDDLE** *Bollito con patate e zafferano,* boiled beef with potatoes and saffron, served at Trattoria il Maestro del Brodo, Palermo. **BOTTOM** Butcher case at Capo Market, one of the historical outdoor markets in Palermo. *Involtini alla siciliana,* skewered meat rolls shown on the right, are popular in Sicily. Thin slices of meat are rolled around a mixture of toasted bread crumbs, pine nuts, currants and cheese, skewered and grilled.

TOP LEFT Chef Salvatore Cascino with a plate of fish rolls, *involtini di pesce,* prepared for grilling at Ristorante La Botte, Monreale. **TOP RIGHT** Small grocery store in Castelbuono. Shopkeepers typically stack crates of produce outside because of limited shelf space inside. **BOTTOM** *Involtini di melanzane con spaghetti,* slices of eggplant wrapped around spaghetti, served at Ristorante La Pigna, San Giovanni La Punta.

TOP LEFT Forming *caciocavallo,* a mild cow's milk cheese that is stretched and shaped by hand into a pear shape with a knob on top. **TOP RIGHT** Mimma and Mercurio Carbone baking hand-made traditional round bread, *muffuletta,* in their wood-burning oven in Piana degli Albanesi. **MIDDLE** *Sedanini ai frutti di mare,* seafood with pasta named "little celery pieces" because of its resemblance to celery stalks, cooked at Ristorante Sicilia in Bocca alla Marina, Catania. **BOTTOM** *Polpette in foglia di limone,* veal meatballs wrapped in lemon leaves, served at Azienda Agricola Trinità, an *agriturismo* in Mascalucia.

TOP LEFT *Carpaccio di zucchine,* marinated zucchini slices, served at Azienda Agricola Trinità, an *agriturismo* in Mascalucia. **TOP RIGHT** *Linguine all'aragosta,* linguine with lobster, served at Trattoria il Delfino, Sferracavallo. **MIDDLE LEFT** *Antipasti* (appetizers) served at Trattoria del Pescatore, San Leone. **MIDDLE RIGHT** *Cannoli,* fried pastry tubes filled with sweet ricotta cream, at Bar Elena, Piana degli Albanesi. **BOTTOM** *Carciofi,* artichokes. The small purple ones are especially prized.

TOP LEFT Chef Saverio Patti with a dish of pasta with cauliflower, *pasta con il broccolò,* served at Antica Stazione, Ficuzza. **TOP RIGHT** Chef Mariano Carbonetti with meat rolls grilled on skewers, *involtini alla siciliana,* served at Antica Stazione, Ficuzza. **BOTTOM** Assortment of sweets including marzipan fruit made at La Pasticceria di Maria Grammatico, Erice.

TOP LEFT Elaborately painted donkey carts, one shown here in miniature, were a means of transportation for peasants until the 1960s. **TOP RIGHT** Chef Vicenzo Candiano with *dolci del ragusano,* a dessert he created to showcase Ragusa cheese, in the restaurant Locanda Don Serafino, Ragusa Ibla. **MIDDLE LEFT** *Arance alla sagra di Ribera,* an appetizer featuring Ribera's noteworthy oranges, at the Ristorante Leon d'Oro, San Leone. **BOTTOM** Fresh fish and seafood, which are abundant and esteemed in Sicily.

TOP LEFT Chef Peppe Barone of Fattoria delle Torri, Modica, with *tortelli di fave cottoie di modica su ragu di maiale al cioccolato,* a dish he created to feature local products (a fava bean variety, pork from black pigs of the Nebrodi Forest and chocolate from Modica). **TOP RIGHT** Chef Giovanni Farruggio with a pasta dish using pistachios from Bronte, *pennette con pesto di pistacchio e mandorle,* at the Ristorante La Pigna, San Giovanni La Punta. **BOTTOM** Inviting outdoor dining area at the Ristorante La Pigna, San Giovanni La Punta.

TOP *Mousse di ricotta,* ricotta mousse topped with caramelized sugar and served with chocolate sauce, Al Fogher Ristorante, Piazza Armerina. **MIDDLE LEFT** Maria Grammatico holding one of her famous Easter lambs meticulously sculpted of marzipan by hand, at La Pasticceria di Maria Grammatico, Erice. **MIDDLE RIGHT** Each Easter lamb made at La Pasticceria di Maria Grammatico is unique. **BOTTOM** Fruit and vegetable stall in the old market in the the lively Borgo Vecchio quarter, Palermo.

peperonata sweet peppers, cut into pieces and stir-fried with tomatoes and sliced onions.

peperoni arrostiti sweet peppers that have been roasted (preferably over hot coals), peeled, cut into strips and dressed with olive oil, garlic and chopped parsley.   GOOD CHOICE

peperoni ripieni stuffed sweet peppers filled with a mixture of toasted bread crumbs, pine nuts, currants and cheese, then baked.   EXCELLENT

peperoni sott'olio pickled sweet peppers packed in oil.

pesce spada affumicato smoked swordfish.

pesce spada alla marinara swordfish cooked with tomatoes, capers and olives. Also called *pesce spada alla matalotta, pesce spada alla ghiotta* or p*esce spada alla messinese.*

pesce spada alla palermitana breaded swordfish, stir-fried or grilled. Also called *pesce spada panato* or *impanato.*

pesce spada arrosto grilled swordfish.   GOOD CHOICE

pesce stocco con cipolle dried cod with onions, typical of the province of Messina. Also called *stoccafisso con cipolle.*

pesto all'usticese pesto in the style of the island of Ustica. It is similar to *pesto trapanese,* but with capers instead of almonds.

pesto di melanzane eggplant pesto, made from grilled eggplant, olive oil and salt, used as a spread for antipasti.

pesto di pistacchio pistachio pesto, which is excellent for dressing pasta. This sauce, made with pistachios grown near the town of Bronte, is sold in major Sicilian cities and is increasingly popular.   LOCAL FAVORITE

pesto trapanese Trapani-style pesto with basil, plenty of garlic (one clove per person), chopped raw tomatoes and almonds. It is used to dress pasta, especially *busiati* (see *Food & Flavors Guide*).   LOCAL FAVORITE

piedini di maiale pig's feet, boiled and sold in historical markets.

pietrafennula (Sic) very hard, stick-shaped nougat, made with ground peels of oranges and citrons and cooked with honey, cinnamon and vanilla. These sweets, which used to be typical of Carnival time, are difficult to find today.

pignoccata (Sic) pyramid of small, round fritters dipped in honey. Its name derives from *pigna* ("pine cone"), an ancient Mediterranean fertility symbol. It is a sweet typical of Carnival. Messina has its own version of the *pignoccata,* which is sold at Christmas. One side is covered with chocolate icing, the other with vanilla- and lemon-flavored sugar. Also called *pignolata.*   LOCAL FAVORITE

pittinnicchi (Sic) small pieces of the ribs of a very young kid. The small quantity of meat that is attached to the ribs is considered particularly good by connoisseurs, who prefer to eat it with their fingers.

pizza margherita pizza with mozzarella cheese and tomatoes.

GOOD CHOICE **pizza napoletana** classic Neapolitan pizza with mozzarella cheese, tomatoes, and anchovy fillets on top. Pizza is believed to have been born in the city of Naples.

pizza quattro stagioni "four seasons pizza" with artichokes, mushrooms, ham, cheese and tomato.

pizza rianata (Sic) pizza sprinkled with plenty of oregano. Also called simply *rianata*.

polenta di cicerchie polenta made using flour from the legume called *cicerchie* rather than cornmeal. The dish is a specialty of the province of Enna.

GOOD CHOICE **polipetti in umido** stew of baby octopus cooked with tomatoes, olive oil, and garlic. Also called *polipetti murati, polipetti in tegame, moscardini in umido* or *maiolini in umido*.

polipo bollito (lesso) boiled octopus, sometimes sold in street stalls. Baby octopus is especially popular. Also called *polpo bollito (lesso)* and *purpu bollito (lesso)* in Sicilian. See *Foods & Flavors Guide* for the distinction between *bollito* and *lesso*.

pollo alla cacciatora braised chicken, hunter's-style, with a sauce of tomatoes, sometimes with mushrooms.

pollo arrosto rotisserie chicken, typically sold in shops that specialize in selling whole roasted chickens with potatoes. Chicken is eaten in the home, but usually is considered too ordinary to be served in Sicilian restaurants.

polpette di baccalà fried balls made of shredded salted cod mixed with boiled mashed potatoes. This is a very common dish in Spain and may have originated there. It is a specialty of Messina.

polpette di carne meatballs. Ground beef is mixed with eggs, grated cheese, nutmeg and stale bread moistened with milk, then formed into balls and fried. They may be eaten plain, cooked in tomato sauce (*al sugo*), or, more rarely, wrapped in lemon leaves (*foglie di limone*) and baked. (See *Recipes,* p. 56.)

polpette di finocchietto vegetarian balls or patties, in which chopped wild fennel leaves substitute for meat.

polpette di gallina chicken meatballs, usually served in stock with broken spaghetti (*tagliolini*). This dish traditionally is served at Easter and Christmas in the town of Modica.

polpette di melanzane vegetarian balls or patties, in which mashed eggplant substitutes for meat.

SICILIAN CLASSIC **polpette di neonata** fried patties of newborn sardines or *vope* (a local fish similar to bogue) mixed with beaten egg. Also called *polpette di novellame*.

polpette di sarde patties of chopped fresh sardines, a Palermitan speciality. See *polpette di tonno*.

polpette di tonno tuna patties. In the province of Trapani, and especially in the Egadi Islands, this dish is prepared with finely chopped fresh tuna mixed with bread crumbs, pine nuts and currants. The patties are cooked in fresh tomato sauce. Fresh sardines are used to make the similar *polpette di sarde* in Palermo.   LOCAL FAVORITE

polpettone large ground-beef roll. A mixture of ground beef, eggs, grated cheese and stale bread moistened with milk is shaped into a roll around whole (shelled) hard-boiled eggs. The roll is browned in oil then cooked in tomato sauce.

polpo bollito (lesso) boiled octopus. See *polipo bollito*.

pomodori ripieni tomatoes, either fresh or sun-dried, stuffed with a mixture of toasted bread crumbs, pine nuts, currants and diced cheese and baked.

pupi 'a cena (Sic) sugar statuettes. See *pupi di zucchero*.   SICILIAN CLASSIC

pupi di zucchero gaudily colored sugar statuettes meant for children for All Souls' Day (November 2nd). Knights and ballerinas are two popular characters. Also called *pupi 'a cena*.   SICILIAN CLASSIC

pupo cull'ova (Sic) Easter cookie shaped like a big gingerbread man. Like many other traditional Easter sweets, the *pupo cull'ova* is baked with an unshelled hard-boiled egg inside. The name literally means "doll with the egg."

purpu (Sic) bollito (lesso) boiled octopus. See *polipo bollito*.

quaresimali Lenten almond cookies (Lent is *Quaresima* in Italian). These delicious biscotti originated as a special treat to be eaten during Lent, but are now available at any time of year.

quarume (Sic) the soft intestines, upper part of the stomach and other interior parts of cow (except spleen, pancreas and gall bladder), which are boiled and sold in the historical markets.

ravioli di cernia al ragù di pesce ravioli filled with grouper and dressed with fish sauce.   WONDERFUL

ravioli di ricotta al ragù ravioli filled with ricotta cheese and dressed with a pork ragout. Also called *ravioli di ricotta al sugo di maiale*.   GOOD CHOICE

ravioli di ricotta dolci ravioli filled with sweet ricotta cream and fried. They are similar to *cassatelle di ricotta*.

LOCAL FAVORITE **ravioli panteschi** ravioli filled with ricotta cheese and chopped mint, and dressed with fresh tomato sauce, a specialty of the island of Pantelleria.

raviolone pasta roll filled with ricotta and spinach. See *rollò di ricotta e spinaci*.

reginelle sesame seed–covered cookies. See *biscotti regina*.

rianata (Sic) pizza sprinkled with plenty of oregano. Also called *pizza rianata*.

SICILIAN CLASSIC **ricotta al forno** baked ricotta cheese. Blocks of ricotta cheese, sometimes in particular shapes, are baked in the oven until the crust becomes brown.

ricotta fritta fresh ricotta cheese, cut into rectangles, breaded and fried.

GOOD CHOICE **risotto alla marinara** risotto with seafood. It is the only risotto preparation common in Sicily, where rice is not commonly used. Also called *risotto ai frutti di mare*.

rognoni in tegame stewed lamb or beef kidneys.

LOCAL FAVORITE **rollò di Caltanissetta** cake made from a chocolate and almond-flour dough rolled with a filling of sweet ricotta cheese and marzipan. It is a specialty of Caltanissetta in the province of Caltanissetta, where, in 2002, pastry chefs in the main square prepared a *rollò* 303 meters long, establishing a Guinness World Record for longest *rollò* (rolled sweet).

rollò di ricotta e spinaci large, round piece of boiled pasta dough, covered with a layer of fresh ricotta cheese and chopped spinach, rolled up and cooked in tomato sauce. Also called *raviolone*.

rosolio homemade cordial made from macerated fruits or herbs. A *rosolio* may be offered with dessert.

salame di capra goat-meat salami, a rare specialty from the Madonie Mountains.

salame di cinghiale salami made from wild boar meat.

salame turco Turkish salami, a dessert. A mixture of broken cookies, nuts, melted butter, milk, eggs, sugar and cocoa is shaped into a roll, chilled and sliced. The pieces of cookie and nuts look like the chunks of meat and fat in a salami.

salmoriglio sauce of olive oil with chopped garlic, oregano, parsley, lemon juice and salt, used to moisten grilled fish. See *ammogghiu*.

salsa verde green sauce made from chopped parsley mixed with oil and vinegar. It normally accompanies boiled meat, but it is also very good on boiled artichokes, and on ripe, raw tomatoes.

salsiccia al ragù sausage cooked with wine and tomato sauce.

salsiccia arrosto grilled sausage. High-quality pork sausage, usually flavored with wild fennel seeds, is produced by butchers in most Sicilian towns. Sausage often is served with local wild greens (see *verdure amare, Foods & Flavors Guide*).

salsiccia di cinghiale arrosto grilled wild-boar sausage.

salsiccia secca dry sausage. Sliced like a salami, it is a popular traditional food, served as an antipasto.

sanguinaccio "sausage" made of pig's blood. The sweet version is made with sugar, raisins and chocolate. Formerly homemade or sold on the streets, *sanguinaccio* is difficult to find today.

sarago arrosto grilled white bream.

sarde a beccafico rolls of fresh sardines stuffed with a filling of   SICILIAN CLASSIC
bread crumbs, pine nuts and currants. The sardines must be butterflied, which every Sicilian fishmonger does for his customers. The *beccafico* ("fig picker") is a songbird that eats figs, to which the sardine rolls bear some resemblance. Scabbard fish may substitute for sardines in this classic Sicilian dish.

sarde arrosto grilled fresh sardines.

sarde fritte deep-fried fresh, butterflied sardines.   VERY GOOD

savoiardi oval, dry cookies with thin, white, icing. The name suggests an origin in Savoy, a French region bordering northern Italy. In Aidone in the province of Enna, *savoiardi* are round and are called *gemelle* ("twins").

scacce (Sic) bread rolls stuffed like a strudel with cheese,   LOCAL FAVORITE
tomatoes, eggplants or other vegetables, sold in various sizes at coffee bars and *rosticcerie,* especially in Ragusa and Syracuse.

scaccio (Sic) popular name for the nuts and seeds that Sicilians   SICILIAN CLASSIC
love to munch. It is a popular street food.

scamorza fusa *scamorza* cheese melted on a grill. *Scamorza* is similar to mozzarella, but saltier.

scorfani in umido large, scaled, scorpion fish stewed in a small   VERY GOOD
quantity of tomato sauce. The sauce is obtained by cooking a few fresh, diced tomatoes in olive oil, in which abundant garlic has been previously browned.

semifreddo alle mandorle almond ice cream. Cream is the   YUMMY
foundation of this recently introduced and increasingly popular ice cream. Also called *parfait di mandorle.*

seppie in tegame "cuttlefish in the pot." Cuttlefish stew with tomatoes, olive oil, and garlic. Also called *seppie in umido.*

seppie ripiene cuttlefish stuffed with toasted bread crumbs, pine   EXCELLENT
nuts and currants.

LOCAL FAVORITE **seppioline fritte** fried baby cuttlefish. Also called *cappuccetti* ("little hoods") *fritti* because of their shape.

LOCAL FAVORITE **sfinci (Sic)** fritters. They can be sweet (if filled with fresh ricotta cream) or savory (if filled with anchovy fillets). They are western Sicily's counterpart to Catania's *crespelle,* and traditionally are prepared at home for the Eve of the Feast of the Immaculate Conception (December 7th) and Christmas Eve (December 24th). Very large sweet *sfinci* (*sfinci di San Giuseppe*) are made for the feast of St. Joseph (March 19th). In the Aeolian Islands there are *sfinci d'ova* made with egg in the batter. Occasionally (for example, at Carnival in Mezzojuso in the province of Palermo) potatoes are used in the *sfinci* batter.

LOCAL FAVORITE **sfincione** Palermitan pizza, topped with tomato sauce, onions, *caciocavallo* cheese, toasted bread crumbs and oregano. Most pizzas in Sicily are thin and baked in the brick oven in pizzerias, which open only in the evening, but *sfincione* is thick and available at most bakeries in Palermo at any time of the day. The large quantity of onions on *sfincione* makes it suitable only for strong stomachs.

LOCAL FAVORITE **sfogliatelle** Neapolitan layered pastry (*sfoglia*) filled with ricotta cream. In the Madonie Mountains *sfogliatelle* are completely different—a small version of a cake called *sfoglio*. See *sfoglio*.

sfoglio cake filled with a mixture of chocolate, sugar and grated *tuma* cheese, typical of the Madonie Mountains.

sformato Italian quiche made without cream and with less butter than French quiche. The filling may be based on béchamel sauce or fresh ricotta cheese.

sformato di fagiolini fresh bean quiche. See *sformato*.

sformato di spinaci spinach quiche. See *sformato*.

sgroppino lemon *gelato* shaken with *limoncello* liqueur.

spaghetti allo scoglio spaghetti dressed with a sauce made with a few tomatoes and fish that have been caught on the rocks (*scoglio*) near the coast.

SICILIAN CLASSIC **spaghetti con bottarga** spaghetti with grated, salted tuna roe (*bottarga*), olive oil and garlic. A few tomatoes may enhance the flavor of this dish.

spaghetti con cozze spaghetti with mussels. It may be prepared with or without tomato sauce.

GREAT **spaghetti con fave e piselli** spaghetti with fresh peas and fava beans. Fresh ricotta cheese may be added to this dish.

spaghetti con frutti di mare spaghetti with tomato sauce and a variety of seafoods.

spaghetti con il nero di seppia spaghetti with black cuttlefish ink.   SICILIAN CLASSIC

spaghetti con neonata spaghetti with baby fish.

spaghetti con ricci spaghetti with raw sea-urchin gonads, olive oil   SICILIAN CLASSIC
and garlic. A few cherry tomatoes may enhance the flavor of
this dish, which has become incredibly popular.

spaghetti con sugo di castrato spaghetti with a sauce made of
tomatoes and *castrato,* meat from a sheep that has been castrated
to make it more tender.

spaghetti con vongole spaghetti with tomato sauce and clams.

spaghetti con vongole in bianco spaghetti with clams, garlic,   GREAT
parsley and olive oil, but without tomato sauce; hence, *in bianco*
("in white"). Two kinds of clams are available in Sicily. The ones
with a darker shell are called *vongole veraci* ("true clams"), and
are reputed to have a better taste. When these clams are used to
make this dish, it may be called *spaghetti con vongole veraci.*

spaghetti in brodo di aragosta spaghetti cut in small pieces and
cooked in a rather liquid lobster sauce. It is a specialty of
Trapani and the Egadi Islands.

spatola fritta fried fillet of scabbard fish.

spezzatino di agnello lamb stew with potatoes and green peas.   GOOD CHOICE

spezzatino di carne beef stew with potatoes and green peas.

spicchitedda (Sic) Christmas cookies typical of the Aeolian   LOCAL FAVORITE
islands (especially Salina), sweetened with *vino cotto,* grapes
boiled down into "cooked wine."

spiedini alla siciliana Sicilian skewered meat rolls. See *involtini
alla siciliana.*

spigola arrosto grilled sea bass.

spumini hazelnut cookies typical of the town of Montalbano
Elicona in the province of Palermo.

spumoni a very foamy kind of ice cream.

stigghiola (stigliole) (Sic) intestines from lambs and kids, washed,
and wrapped around stalks of parsley. In Palermo they are
grilled in the streets, where they emit a characteristic pungent
smell. In the province of Agrigento *stigghiola* is a dish of lamb
intestines with liver, hard-boiled eggs and onions.

stinco di maiale al forno pork shank baked whole (bone included).

stoccafisso alla messinese Messina-style dried cod. It is cooked   LOCAL FAVORITE
with a few tomatoes, capers and olives. Messina, being the
Sicilian city closest to the continent, has imported dried cod
(*pesce stocco*) from Norway (where it is called *stokfisk*) since
medieval times, while the rest of Sicily typically makes do with
the cheaper *baccalà,* salted cod. Also called *stoccafisso alla ghiotta.*

stoccafisso con cipolle dried cod with onions, especially typical of the town of Novara di Sicilia. Also called *pesce stocco con cipolle.*

stracotto di maiale al sugo braised pork in tomato sauce. It is called *stracotto* ("overcooked") because it is cooked so long.

LOCAL FAVORITE **tagliancozzi** almond biscuits typical of the town of Marsala. They are an ideal accompaniment to the famous Marsala wine. *Tagliancozzi* are similar to *quaresimali* (see this *Guide*).

tagliatelle con ricotta e spinaci long ribbon noodles (*tagliatelle*) with ricotta cheese and spinach. In the countryside the dish may be made with wild greens such as borage instead of spinach.

taralli dry biscuits the size and shape of a doughnut, flavored with aniseed and covered with white icing.

LOCAL FAVORITE **testa di turco** "Turk's head," a turban-shaped dessert. In some towns it is like a giant beignet filled with sweet ricotta cream. In Castelbuono *testa di turco* is a lasagna-like sweet, with layers of fried dough and custard flavored with cinnamon and lemon. In Scicli in the province of Ragusa it traditionally is made for the feast of the Madonna della Milizie on the last Sunday of May.

tetù (Sic) dry cookies made from the leftover dough scraped from the pastry shop's baking pans. Together with *rosolio* cordial and *taralli* biscuits, *tetù* used to be the traditional treat for engagement and christening parties.

EXCELLENT **timballo di capellini** a molded dish or timbale made with angel-hair pasta and meat ragout. This aristocratic counterpart of *anelletti al forno* has a buttery dressing.

tonno affumicato smoked tuna.

GREAT **tonno al ragù** large pieces of fresh tuna incised with garlic and mint leaves, browned in olive oil, cooked in tomato sauce, sliced and served hot. Also called *tonno ammuttunato* ("stuffed tuna") in Sicilian.

tonno con cipolle fresh boiled tuna, served cold and dressed with vinegar, capers and plenty of onions that have been browned in olive oil. Also called *cipollata di tonno.*

tonno in agrodolce sweet-and-sour tuna. It is similar to *tonno con cipolle,* but includes sugar.

torrone nougat, a candy typically made from honey, egg whites, sugar and nuts. *Torrone* can be rather brittle (*torrone duro*) or soft and chewy (*torrone morbido*). Torrone from Caltanissetta is especially famous. See *cubbaita.*

torta gelato gelato layered with sponge cake and decorated like a **YUMMY**
cake. It is available in various flavors at *gelaterie* in the summer.

torta setteveli "cake of the seven veils." Layers of sponge cake **YUMMY**
and chocolate characterize this recent invention, widely available
in the Palermo area.

totani arrosto grilled *totani,* a mollusk very similar to squid.

triaca a'pasta (Sic) fresh bean soup served in Catania. See *minestra
di fagioli freschi.*

triglie alla livornese red mullet Livorno-style, cooked with a few
tomatoes, capers and olives. Sicilians cook many kinds of fish in
this style, which is also called *alla ghiotta* ("glutton-style").

triglie fritte fried red mullet. **GREAT**

trippa al pomodoro tripe with tomato sauce; also called *trippa al
ragù.*

trippa alla palermitana Palermo-style tripe. Slices of cooked tripe,
fried eggplant and cheese are layered with tomato sauce and then
baked. Also called *trippa con parmigiana.*

uva al liquore liquor-flavored grapes. This dessert, which
requires at least a week to prepare, has almost disappeared
from the city of Messina, where it was once a specialty.

verdure grigliate medley of vegetables, grilled on a hot slab or
over coals. Also called *verdure alla piastra.*

verdure in pastella vegetables (commonly cauliflower and
cardoons) dipped in a thick, yeasty batter, and then deep-fried.
Sage leaves and wild cardoons found in mountain areas can be
cooked in the same manner.

vitello tonnato sliced veal in tuna and mayonnaise sauce. It is
served cold or at room temperature. This dish is not Sicilian. It
arrived on the tables of upper middle-class Sicilian families
from France and Northern Italy in relatively recent times.

vurrania (Sic) bollita boiled wild borage. Borage is *vurrania* in
Sicilian, *borragine* in Italian.

zucca all'agrodolce sweet-and-sour preparation of winter squash. **SICILIAN CLASSIC**
See *fegato ai Sette Cannoli,* this *Guide.*

zucchine ripiene stuffed zucchini. Zucchini are cut in half lengthwise and stuffed with a mixture of toasted bread crumbs, pine nuts, currants and sliced cheese.

GOOD CHOICE **zuppa di cozze** sea mussel stew. A few tomatoes are diced and cooked in olive oil in which garlic has been sautéed. The mussels are added and cooked until they open. Croutons are often served for dipping in the sauce. A simple version without tomatoes is called *cozze scoppiate* or *impepata di cozze*.

zuppa di crastuna (Sic) soup made from large land snails.

zuppa di legumi legume soup. It may be made with beans, chickpeas, lentils or a mixture of legumes.

GOOD CHOICE **zuppa di pesce** "fish soup," though it is so much more. The soup begins with diced tomatoes cooked in olive oil in which garlic has been sautéed. Different kinds of shellfish and fish (with bones, head and tail) are added to the tomatoes. Croutons are often served for dipping in the sauce. This soup usually is a main course, or *piatto unico*, meaning that it functions as both the first and second course at a given meal, especially since generous portions are served.

LOCAL FAVORITE **zuzzu (Sic)** butcher's pork scraps, such as cartilage, cut into small pieces, put in gelatin and cut into squares. It is a specialty of the Catania province, particularly of the town of Linguaglossa.

Foods & Flavors Guide

This chapter contains a comprehensive list of foods, spices, kitchen utensils and cooking terminology in Italian, with English translations. Terms in Sicilian or in regional Italian dialect, designated by (Sic), are given instead of or in addition to their Italian counterparts when their usage is common in Sicily.

Singular and plural forms of nouns are given when both are used. In general, singular feminine nouns end in *-a,* their plurals in *-e;* singular masculine nouns end in *-o,* their plurals in *-i.* However, to confuse the issue, many Italian words, both feminine and masculine, end in *-e* in the singular and *-i* in the plural. When words are used primarily in the singular or plural sense, only the form commonly used will be listed. If the change from singular to plural only involves the last letter, just this letter change in the plural form is indicated. For example, we list *oliva (e)* rather than *oliva (olive).* If more than the last letter changes in the plural, the entire plural form is included, as in *acciuga (acciughe).* For simplicity, the singular and plural forms are included only in the first item of a series. For example, both forms are given for melon, but not for winter melon and yellow melon. Adjectives are listed only in the masculine singular form, again for simplicity. However, please note that adjective endings do change to reflect gender and number.

The *Foods & Flavors Guide* will be helpful in interpreting menus and for shopping in the outdoor markets. You will find that prices are indicated on food in the markets, but the items may not be identified. If you don't recognize something, why not inquire, "What is this called?" (see *Helpful Phrases,* p. 77), and use this *Guide* to help identify it.

a piacere prepared to your choosing.
abbrustolito toasted. Another word for toasted is *tostato.*
acciuga (acciughe) Mediterranean anchovy (*Engraulis encrasicholus*). Anchovies also are called *alacce, alici, anciova* and, in Catania, *masculini.*
acerbo sour, a term primarily used for fruit or vegetables that are unripe. Other words for sour are *agro* and *aspro.*

aceto vinegar.

aceto balsamico balsamic vinegar, a dark, concentrated, aged vinegar made from the cooked and fermented juice of the white grape variety Trebbiano.

acetosa garden sorrel (*Rumex acetosa*). The sour leaves of this herb are used in soups, salads and sauces. *Acetosella* is another variety (*Rumex acetosella*).

acqua water.

acqua brillante tonic water. Also called *acqua tonica.*

acqua con ghiaccio ice water.

acqua di seltz seltzer water; soda water.

acqua fredda cold water.

acqua frizzante carbonated water. Also called *acqua gasata.*

acqua minerale mineral water.

acqua naturale plain bottled water. Also called *acqua non gasata.*

affettato sliced. *Affettati* are sliced cold meats.

affogato poached.

affumicato smoked.

aglassato glazed; glazed look of food due to caramelization.

aglio garlic.

aglio e olio with garlic and olive oil. Also called *all'aglio e olio.*

agnello lamb. Suckling lamb is called *agnellino di latte.*

agro sour. Another word for sour is *aspro.* Also see *acerbo,* this *Guide.*

agrodolce sweet and sour.

agrumi general term for citrus fruits.

ai (al, all', alla) in the style of.

ajola (ajula) striped bream (*Lithognathus mormyrus*).

al burro cooked in butter.

al dente "to the tooth," referring primarily to pasta that is tender on the outside but still has a little "bite" in the center because it is not quite done.

al forno oven-baked.

al guanciale cooked with pork jowl bacon.

al nero di calamaro (al nero di seppia) with squid or cuttlefish ink, which turns a dish black.

al pomodoro with tomato sauce.

al prezzemolo with parsley.

al punto (meat cooked) medium.

al sangue (meat cooked) very rare.

al sugo with sauce or juice.

alaccia (e) Mediterranean anchovy (*Engraulis encrasicolus*). See *acciuga.*

albicocca (albicocche) apricot.

albume egg white; also called *bianco d'uovo* and *chiara d'uovo.*

alfredo with butter, cheese and cream sauce.

alice (i) Mediterranean anchovy (*Engraulis encrasicholus*). See *acciuga.*

alimentari small grocery stores.

alla bava prepared with butter and melted cheese.

alla bolognese with tomato and meat sauce.

alla brace grilled over charcoal.

alla cacciatora hunter's style, braised with tomatoes and sometimes mushrooms.

alla campagnola country-style.

alla carbonara sauce with pancetta, eggs, pecorino cheese and black pepper.

alla carne with meat, most likely beef.

alla casalinga home-style; homemade.

alla contadina farmer's-style.

alla fiamma flamed.

alla ghiotta "glutton style." In fish preparations it implies the inclusion of tomatoes, olives and capers.

alla graticola grilled; broiled.

alla griglia grilled; food cooked on a grill. Another term for grilled is *grigliato.*

alla marinara with fish or seafood.

alla matalotta stewed in tomatoes, olives and capers.

alla milanese Milanese-style, breaded and deep-fried.

alla mugnaia miller's style; fish dishes sautéed in butter and dressed with lemon juice and parsley. This method is called *meunière* in French.

alla Norma generally refers to a dish, typically pasta, served with eggplant, tomato, basil and crumbled *ricotta salata* cheese.

alla palermitana normally refers to breaded, grilled meat.

alla panna served in a creamy sauce of butter, cream and grated cheese.

alla parmigiana with Parmesan cheese and tomatoes.

all'agro dressing with abundant lemon juice.

all'aperto (dining) outdoors.

all'arrabbiata with hot red chile peppers.

alle vongole in clam sauce.

alloro (i) bay leaf. Also called *foglia d'alloro.*

amarena (e) sour cherry.

amaretto Italian almond liqueur.

amaro bitter; also the name of a bitter digestive liqueur, normally sipped after dinner. Averna is the most famous Sicilian brand of this liqueur.

amatriciana pasta sauce made with *pancetta* and tomatoes.

analcolico (i) non-alcoholic drinks.

ananas pineapple.

anciova (Sic) Mediterranean anchovy (*Engraulis encrasicholus*). See *acciuga*.

anelli (anelletti, anellini) ring-shaped pasta.

aneto dill.

anguilla (e) common eel; also called *anguidda* (Sic). Also see *grongo,* this *Guide*.

anice anise. Also an anise-flavored alcohol (called *zammù* in Sicilian). A few drops are added to cold drinking water to make a refreshing summer drink.

animella (e) sweetbread, the thymus gland or pancreas.

anitra (e) duck. Wild duck is *anitra selvatica*.

antipasti a piacere antipasti of one's own choice.

antipasto (i) appetizer. Antipasti can be almost meals in themselves.

arachide (i) peanuts. Also called *noccioline*.

aragosta (e) spiny or rock lobster, crawfish (*Palinurus vulgaris*). Sicilians usually use this same term to refer to the true lobster (*Homarus gammarus*), although the Italian word for the true lobster is *astice*.

arancia (arance) orange.

arancia sanguinella blood orange. Other varieties include *moro* and *tarocco*.

aricciola amberjack (*Seriola dumerili*). See *ricciola,* this *Guide*.

aringa (aringhe) herring. Smoked herring is *aringa affumicata*.

arista (arista di maiale, arista di suino) pork loin.

arrosti misti freddi assortment of cold roasted meats.

arrosto roast or grill; roasted or grilled. Another word for roasted is *arrostito*.

asciutto dry; drained. *Pasta asciutta* has been drained and mixed with sauce.

asparago (i) asparagus.

aspro sour. Another word for sour is *agro*. Also see *acerbo,* this *Guide*.

astice (i) true lobster (*Homarus gammarus*). Sicilians usually call the true lobster *aragosta,* the Italian name for the spiny, or rock lobster.

avena oats.

babbaluci (Sic) small variety of land snail. See *lumaca,* this *Guide*.

bacca (bacche) berry.

bacca di sambuco elderberry.

baccalà salted, dried cod fillets. Before cooking, the fish is soaked in water for a few days to rehydrate it and then rinsed to remove the salt. In the historic street markets, *baccalà* is sold already soaking in pans of water.

bar shop selling spirits, soft drinks and coffee, as well as food items.

barbabietola (e) beet. Also called *bietola*.

basilico basil.

bastarduna (Sic) Smyrna fig, which is highly desirable for its flavor and tender skin. Also used to refer to fruits grown out of season.

bavette long, flat, narrow pasta.

beccaccia woodcock.

beccafico warbler. See *Menu Guide* for a description of *sarde a beccafico*, a sardine dish made to resemble this plump little bird.

ben cotta cooked to well done (meat).

besciamella béchamel sauce, made by whisking milk into a roux.

bevanda (e) drinks; beverages.

bevande comprese cost of drinks included.

bianco white.

bianco d'uovo egg white; also called *albume* and *chiara d'uovo*.

bibita (e) soft drink.

bicchiere drinking glass. Recipes sometimes use *bicchiere* as a unit of measure.

bietola (e) beet (beetroot). Also called *barbabietola*.

birra (e) beer.

birra alla spina draught beer.

birra bionda light beer or ale. Also called *birra chiara*. Dark beer is *birra scura*.

birra in lattina beer in a can.

biscotto (i) dry, twice-baked cookies.

bistecca (bistecche) steak. *Bistecchina* is a thin steak.

bistecca alla fiorentina T-bone steak.

bistecca di manzo beef steak.

bollito boiled; boiled meat. For most Italians, *bollito* and *lesso* are synonyms. Purists make the distinction between foods placed in cold water and boiled (*bollito*) and those placed in boiling water and boiled (*lesso*).

borragine borage; also called *vurrania* in Sicilian.

bottarga salted, pressed roe, typically from the gray mullet or tuna.

bottarga di tonno salted, pressed roe from tuna. Also called *uovo di tonno*.

bottiglia bottle.

braciola (e) meat slice or chop, sometimes rolled around a filling.

braciola di maiale pork chop.

branzino sea bass (*Dicentrarchus labrax* or *Morone labrax*); also called *spigola*.

brasato braised meat.

bresaola thinly sliced, aged, dried, salted beef.

brioche sweet bun.

broccoletti di rape pungent, leafy vegetable with broccoli-like florets.

broccolo (i) (Sic) cauliflower. Broccoli is called *sparacelli* in Sicilian.

brodo broth.

bucatini spaghetti-like pasta with a hole (*buco*) down the center.

budino custard; pudding.

bue (buoi) beef from cattle less than four years old; also see *manzo*.

burro butter. Melted butter is *burro fuso*.

busiati type of fresh pasta shaped by hand by rolling it around a thin stalk or skewer (*buso* means knitting needle) to form a long coil.

cacciagione game.

cachi persimmon. Also called *loti*.

cacio cheese; also called *formaggio*. Grated cheese is *cacio grattato*.

caciocavallo mild cow's milk cheese, stretched and shaped by hand into a pear shape with a knob on top. Its Sicilian name is *cascavaddu*.

cacocciulo (Sic) artichoke; called *carciofo* in Italian.

caffè coffee; also a coffee bar or coffee shop.

caffè americano espresso diluted with hot water.

caffè decaffeinato decaffeinated coffee. The main brand of decaffeinated coffee in Italy is Hag, which often is used as a generic term for decaf.

caffè doppio two espresso servings in one cup. Also called *espresso doppio*.

caffè e latte large cup of hot milk with some coffee.

caffè espresso strong black coffee.

caffè espresso con panna strong black coffee topped with whipped cream.

caffè freddo cold espresso usually served in a small glass.

caffè macchiato espresso topped with foamed milk.

caffè nero black coffee.

caffè ristretto coffee stronger than espresso.

caffetteria (e) coffee shop; bar. Also called *caffè*.

calamari squid. Small squid are *calamaretti*.

caldo warm or hot.

cameriere (i) waiter. A waitress is a *cameriera (e)*.

canditi candied fruits.

canestrato hard, sharp sheep's milk cheese, which is molded in a basket. The cheese has an imprint of the basket on the rind.

cannella cinnamon.

cannellini white kidney beans. Also called *fagioli cannellini*.

cannelloni large pasta tubes, typically stuffed.

cannolicchi razor clams (*Solen vagina*). Also means little *cannoli*.

cantina (e) wine cellar; wine shop.

capelli d'angelo angel hair pasta. It is very similar to *capellini*.

capellini long, fine strands of pasta slightly thicker than angel hair pasta.

capone (i) gurnard fish.

cappero (i) caper, the immature flower bud from the *Capparis spinosa* shrub, which is pickled in vinegar or preserved in salt. Piquant caper buds from the islands of Pantelleria and Salina are packed in sea salt and aged.

cappuccino (i) espresso served with steamed milk, usually served at breakfast.

capra (e) goat. A young goat, or kid, is *capretto (i)*.

caprino (i) goat's-milk cheese.

caramello caramel. Caramelized is *caramellato*.

carciofo (i) artichoke; also called *cacocciulo* (Sic). *Carciofino* is baby artichoke.

cardo (i) cardoon, domesticated thistle, a relative of the artichoke. The celery-like stalks are eaten.

carne meat. Raw meat is *carne cruda*.

carne di cervo venison. Also called *selvaggina* (game).

carne macinata ground meat; also called *carne tritata, capuliato* (Sic) and *capoliato* (Sic). Also see *tritato di manzo*.

carne suina pork.

carnezzeria (Sic) butcher shop. The Italian word for butcher shop is *macelleria*.

carota (e) carrot.

carruba (e) carob pod.

carta menu, in the restaurant setting; otherwise means paper.

carvi caraway; *grani di carvi* is caraway seeds.

casalingo homemade. Another word for homemade is *casareccio. Casalinga*, the feminine of *casalingo*, also means housewife.

cascavaddu Sicilian name for *caciocavallo* cheese. See *caciocavallo*, this *Guide*.

castagna (e) chestnut.

castrato meat from a sheep castrated to make the meat more tender.

cavallo (i) horse; *carne di cavallo* is horse meat.

cavati shell-shaped pasta with rolled-in edges. Large *cavati* are *cavatoni;* small ones are *cavatelli*.

caviale caviar.

cavoletti di Bruxelles Brussels sprouts.

cavolfiore (i) green cauliflower. Sicilians generally call cauliflower *broccolo*.

cavolfiore violetto light-purple cauliflower.

cavolo (i) cabbage.

ceci chickpeas, typically used dried.

cedro (i) citron (*Citrus medica*), a knobby, yellow citrus fruit related to the lemon, but less sour. The *cedro* is larger and its pulp and pith are tasty. It is sold in the streets as a snack. A large citron is called *pipittuna* in Sicilian.

cefalo (i) gray mullet (*Mugil cephalus*). Also called *muggine*. The eggs of the female, still encased in a membrane, are salted, sun-dried and covered in wax to make the delicacy called *bottarga*. See *bottarga*, this *Guide*.

cena (e) evening meal.

cernia (e) grouper (*Epinephelus guaza*).

cervello brain.

cetriolo (i) cucumber. A pickled young cucumber (gherkin) is a *cetriolino* (*i*).

chiara (e) d'uovo egg white; also called *albume* and *bianco d'uovo*.

chiodi di garofano cloves.

ciabatta (e) coarse bread with a soft, porous texture.

cicoria chicory.

cicirelli long, thin fish similar to smelt.

ciliegia (e) cherry.

cimino (Sic) sesame seed.

cinghiale (i) wild boar.

cioccolata chocolate. Hot chocolate is *cioccolata calda*.

cipolla (e) onion.

cipolla scalogna scallion.

cipollata describes a dish made with a lot of onions.

coda di rospo monkfish; angler fish (*Lophius spp*). Also called *rana pescatrice*.

colazione breakfast. *Piccola colazione* and *prima colazione* also mean breakfast. In mainland Italy *colazione* means lunch.

coltello (i) knife.

composta jam-like fruit mixture.

compreso included.

con panna with cream.

concentrato di pomodoro tomato concentrate; tomato paste.

conchiglie shell-shaped pasta. The small version is *conchigliette*.

confetteria name of a shop selling candies and confections.

coniglio (i) rabbit. Wild rabbit is *coniglio selvatico*.

cono (i) cone (ice cream).

conserva preserves, jams and jellies; also means cake fillings, and a mixture of chopped nuts and dried figs.

conto (i) check; bill.

contorno (i) side dish; garnish. This typically refers to a vegetable side dish.

controfiletto sirloin.

coperto (i) cover charge (not a tip) added to a restaurant bill.

coppa cup; goblet. Also refers to pork cured in a casing.

corbezzolo (i) small, round, spiky-surfaced red fruit of the strawberry tree (*Arbutus unedo*). It makes a very good, but not commonly found, jam.

coriandolo coriander.

cornetto (i) croissant.

cosciotto (i) di agnello leg of lamb.

cosciotto di maiale leg of pork.

costa (e) rib; also spelled *costola*.

costa di manzo rib roast; short ribs.

costata (e) chop. Another word for chop is *costoletta (e)*.

costate d'agnello rack of lamb.

costata di vitello veal chop. Another term for veal chop is *costoletta di vitello*.

costine di maiale pork spareribs.

costoletta di maiale pork chop.

cotogna (e) quince; also called *mela cotogna*. *Cotognata* is quince paste.

cotoletta (e) cutlet, typically breaded and fried.

cotto cooked.

cotto a puntino medium done.

cotto a vapore steamed; also simply called *a vapore*.

cozze mussels (*Mytilus galloprovincialis*).

crastuna (Sic) large land snail similar to French escargot. See also *lumaca*.

crema da montare whipping cream; also called *panna*. Whipped cream is *panna montata*.

crema gialla custardy pastry cream filling. Also called *crema pasticcera*.

crema pasticcera custardy pastry cream filling. Also called *crema gialla*.

croccante crunchy; also means nut crunch similar to brittle.

crocchetta (e) croquette. Also called *crocchè*.

crostaceo (i) shellfish.

crostata (e) tart; pie.

crudo raw.

crusca bran.

cucchiaio (cucchiaino) spoon.

cucina kitchen; cuisine.

cucina stagionale seasonal cooking.

cucunci caper berries, the mature fruit of the caper shrub (*Capparis spinosa*), which is cultivated in the Aeolian Islands and in Pantelleria. They resemble little cucumbers, and, like the immature buds of the shrub (capers), they are salted and pickled, and sometimes used in cooking. *Cucunci* have a very strong caper flavor. See *cappero*, this *Guide*.

cucuzza (e) Sicilian word for all kinds of squash and zucchini.

cuoco (a) chef; cook.

cuore (i) heart.

cuori di carciofi artichoke hearts.

cuscus couscous. Small pellets made by rubbing semolina flour with water.

dattero (i) date.

del giorno of the day.

della casa house specialty.

dentice dentex (*Dentex dentex*), a saltwater fish similar to sea bream.

di magro meatless.

di stagione in season.

disossato deboned; filleted.

ditali "thimbles;" short, tububular pasta. Large *ditali* are *ditaloni;* small *ditali* are *ditalini;* small, ridged *ditali* are *ditalini rigati.*

DOC *Denominazione di Origine Controllata,* or denomination of controlled origin. It is Italy's system of quality assurance for wines, requiring production within a specified region using defined methods.

dolce (i) dessert; sweet; pastry.

dolcificante artificial sweetener.

DOP *Denominazione di Origine Protetta,* or protected designation of origin, a designation that means that the method of production of a food item is traditional to the location and conforms to high standards.

doppio zero 00 highly refined soft-wheat flour, almost the consistency of talc.

dorato browned; golden brown.

drogheria (e) grocery.

duro hard; tough.

eliche short, spiral pasta. Also called *fusilli.*

enoteca store selling wine, typically with a large assortment of wines.

erba (e) herb.

ericino mint-flavored liqueur from Erice.

espresso doppio two espresso servings in one cup. Also called *caffè doppio.*

espresso macchiato espresso with a small amount of foamy milk on top. Also called *caffè macchiato.*

estratto di pomodoro concentrated, sun-dried tomato paste. Tomatoes are puréed, salted and dried in the sun until thick and leathery. The paste is only available in Sicily and is sold by weight. It is not the same as tomato sauce, *salsa di pomodoro,* or as tomato concentrate, *concentrato di pomodoro. Estratto di pomodoro* is also called *strattu* in Sicilian.

etto unit of weight equal to 100 grams. Fish dishes are frequently served by the *etto,* and typically become an expensive menu choice.

fagiano pheasant.

fagioli beans.

fagioli badda local, bicolor beans found in the region of Polizzi Generosa. White and violet, white and black, and white and light brown varieties exist.

fagioli bianchi di Spagna lima beans.

fagioli borlotti dried tan beans with red streaks.

fagioli cannellini white kidney beans. Also simply called *cannellini.*

fagioli freschi fresh beans.

fagioli rossi red kidney beans.

fagiolini green beans or string beans.

farcito stuffed.

farfalle bow-tie pasta.

farina flour.

farina di granoturco corn flour.

farina gialla cornmeal.

farina rimacinata durum wheat flour (semolina).

fatto in casa homemade.

fattura (e) receipt; also called *ricevuta.*

fava (e) broad bean; fava bean (*Vicia faba*).

favalucieddi (Sic) medium-size land snail. See *lumaca,* this *Guide.*

fave cottoia local variety of fava beans found in the region of Modica.

fave fresche fresh fava beans, available in the spring.

fecola di patate potato flour.

fegato liver.

fegato di vitello calf's liver.

ferretti tubular noodles made by wrapping fresh pasta sheets around a hairpin.

fetta (e) slice. *Fettina (e)* is a small slice.

fianco (fianchi) flank.

fico (fichi) fig. A dried fig is *fico secco.*

fico d'India prickly pear cactus fruit.

filetto (i) fillet.

finocchietto (i) wild fennel. The feathery fronds of the plant are used in cooking. The root or bulb is tiny compared to that of cultivated fennel.

finocchio (i) fennel.

fior di latte mozzarella made with cow's milk.

fiore (i) di zucca zucchini blossoms.

focacceria special shop or stall selling street food.

foglia (e) leaf.

foglia d'alloro bay leaf. Also simply called *alloro*.

forchetta (e) fork.

formaggio (i) cheese. Also called *cacio*. Grated cheese is *formaggio grattugiato*.

formaggio a pasta filata cheese handmade by stretching and kneading the curds before molding the mass into a typical shape. *Pasta filata* cheeses have great elasticity and include provolone, mozzarella and *caciocavallo*.

fragola (e) strawberry. Wild strawberries are *fragole di bosco*.

fragoline di Ribera very small, tasty, cultivated strawberries from Ribera.

frattaglie giblets.

freddo cold.

fresco fresh.

friggitoria (e) snack bar or food stand specializing in fried foods such as *panelle* and *arancine* (see *Menu Guide*).

frittella (e) pancake; fritter. Also the name of an important Sicilian dish with fresh artichokes, peas and fava beans (see *Menu Guide*).

fritto fried.

fritto misto assortment of fried foods. The term usually refers to seafood.

frumento wheat. Whole wheat is *frumento integrale*.

frutta fruit.

frutta di stagione fruit in season.

frutti di bosco berries.

frutti di mare seafood.

funghi di ferla wild mushroom that grows in the microenvironment beneath the foliage of the giant fennel plant (*Ferula communis*), an ornamental member of the fennel family called *ferla* or *ferola* in Italian.

fungo (funghi) mushroom.

fusilli corkscrew-shaped pasta. Also called *eliche*.

galletta (e) simple, dry biscuit.

gallina (e) egg-laying hen.

gamba (e) di vitello veal shank.

gambero (i) shrimp. Tiny shrimp are *gamberetti*. Large shrimp or prawns are *gamberoni*.

gambero (i) imperiale (i) very large prawn (*Penaeus kerathurus*).

gelateria ice cream shop.

gelatina jelly; aspic jelly.

gelso (i) mulberry.

gelsomino (i) jasmine.

ghiaccio ice.

giallo yellow.

giallo (i) d'uovo egg yolk.

girasole sunflower.

girello rump; rump roast.

giri (Sic) Swiss chard.

gisiere (Sic) giblets. The Italian word for giblets is *rigaglia* (*e*).

glassa icing; gravy. Glazed is *glassato*.

gnocchi potato dumplings. Semolina dumplings are *gnocchi di semolina*.

grana padano hard, granular, buttery cheese similar to Parmesan.

granatina drink made with pomegranate juice.

granchio (i) (di mare) crab (*Carcinus mediterraneus*).

granita (e) dessert of flavored, crushed ice.

grano grain; wheat.

grano duro hard durum wheat (*Triticum durum*) used for pasta.

grano saraceno buckwheat.

grano tenero soft wheat (*Triticum aestivum*) primarily used for bread and cake. Flour made from soft wheat ranges from the very white and super fine (00) to whole-wheat flour (*integrale*).

granoturco maize; corn.

grappa clear brandy made from grape skins, pulp and seeds after the juice has been extracted.

grassi vegetali vegetable fats.

grasso fatty; greasy. Also means fat; grease.

graticola grill; also called *griglia*.

gratinato topped with bread crumbs and grated cheese, browned in the oven.

grattugiato grated. Another word for grated is *grattato*.

gratuito free.

griglia grill; also called *graticola*. *Grigliato* means grilled. Another term for grilled is *alla griglia*. *Grigliata* is grilled food.

grissino (i) bread stick.

grongo conger eel (*Conger conger*). Also see *anguilla*, this *Guide*.

guanciale cured pig's cheek.

guarnito garnished.

imbottito stuffed.

impanato breaded.

in agrodolce with a sweet-and-sour sauce or dressing.

in bianco "white" dishes such as pasta or rice with no sauce or seasoning.

in brodo cooked or served in broth.

in camicia poached (eggs).

in fresco chilled. The term is typically applied to wine.

in guazzetto stewed, in reference to fish.

in padella stir-fried.

in tegame describes dishes made in a two-handled pot or *tegame*.

in umido stewed; cooked in a small amount of liquid.

indivia endive. Belgian endive is *indivia belga*.

insaccati salami; sausage.

insalata (e) salad.

integrale whole grain.

involtini thinly sliced meat or fish rolled around a filling.

IVA incluse taxes included. Another way of noting this is *tasse incluse*.

lampone (i) raspberry.

lampuga dolphin fish (*Coryphaena hippurus*); commonly marketed in the United States as mahi-mahi. It is not related to the mammalian dolphin.

lardo aged, cured fatback, the tenderest fat from the back of the pig.

latte milk.

latte di mandorla almond milk, a sweet, milky drink made by diluting a concentrated paste of ground almonds with water.

latte intero whole milk.

latte magro skim milk; also called *latte scremato*.

latteria shop selling milk products and often pastries.

lattuga (lattughe) lettuce. Romaine lettuce is *lattuga romana*.

lattume soft roe, or milt, typically from tuna.

lenticchia (e) lentil.

lessato boiled. Another word for boiled is *lesso*.

lesso boiled; boiled meat. Also see *bollito,* this *Guide.*

limetta lime.

limonata lemonade.

limoncello sweet lemon liqueur.

limone (i) lemon.

lingua tongue.

linguine long, thin, flat pasta ribbons.

liquoroso fortified with more alcohol. Refers almost exclusively to wine.

liscio smooth. Refers to pasta without ridges and whiskey without ice.

lista delle vivande menu; also simply called *lista* and *menu*.

lolli type of large, fresh, homemade pasta made in Modica. It resembles *cavati* but is much larger. It usually is cooked with fava beans.

lombata loin. Also called *lombo*.

lonza cured pork loin.

loti persimmon; also called *cachi*.

luccio (i) pike.

lumaca (lumache) 1. land snail. The smallest variety (*Helix aspera*) is called *babbaluci* in Sicilian. In southeastern Sicily medium-sized snails are called *favalucieddi* (Sic); slightly larger ones are called *vaccareddi* (Sic). 2. pasta shaped like a snail shell.

maccheroni macaroni; generic term for pasta of any shape.

macelleria (e) butcher shop. Also called *carnezzeria* in Sicilian.

macinato ground.

maggiorana sweet marjoram.

magro dish with no meat; lean.

maiale (i) pork. Also called *suino,* which means pork or pig.

maialino suckling pig. Also called *porcellino*.

maiolini baby octopuses with two rows of suckers on their arms.

maionese mayonnaise.

maiorchino hard pecorino cheese with peppercorns, made with raw milk from sheep and goats living in wild pastures in the mountains near Messina.

mais corn.

maltagliati pasta in the shape of flat, elongated diamonds. Originally it was homemade and cut into different, irregular shapes (the word literally means "badly cut"). This pasta is used in vegetable soups.

malvasia sweet wine from the Aeolian Islands.

mandarancio (i) citrus fruit that is a cross between the orange and tangerine.

mandarino (i) tangerine; mandarin orange.

mandorla (e) almond. Bitter almond is *mandorla (e) amara (e)*.

manzo beef. Also see *bue*.

marasca (marasche) wild sour morrello cherry used to make desserts and maraschino liqueur. Also called *visciola*.

Marsala well-known, dark, sweet, fortified wine resembling Port, named for the Sicilian city where it is made.

martorana sweetened almond paste. Also called *pasta reale* and *marzipane*.

mascarpone creamy, soft, easily spread, very rich, fresh cow's milk cheese used in savory dishes and desserts, especially *tiramisù*.

masculini Catanian word for the Mediterranean anchovy (*Engraulis encrasicholus*) caught in a net. See *acciuga*.

maturo ripe.

mazzetto odoroso aromatic herbs, typically thyme, rosemary, sage and parsley, bundled together and used to season soups and stocks.

medaglioni di carne medallions, meat patties or round beef fillets. Sometimes called *nodini,* especially for smaller portion sizes.

medio medium.

mela (e) apple.

melagrana (e) pomegranate.

melanzana (e) eggplant.

melassa molasses.

mele cotogne quince; also simply called *cotogne*.

melone (i) melon; in Sicily it refers to watermelon unless specified.

melone d'inverno winter melon with yellow flesh and a thick, dark green rind.

melone giallo yellow melon.

menta spearmint (*Mentha spicata*). Peppermint (*M. piperita*) is *menta piperita*.

menù a prezzo fisso fixed-price menu.

menù turistico selection of standard, less-expensive dishes from the menu, which is displayed outside the restaurant by law.

mercato del pesce fish market.

merenda (e) mid-morning or late afternoon snack.

merluzzo (i) hake (*Merluccius merluccius*); also called *nasello*.

metà half.

mezzo cotto half-cooked, or medium-done. Also means half.

miele honey.

miglio millet.

milza spleen.

minestra soup; also called *zuppa*.

mirto myrtle (*Myrtus communis*); also a liqueur of the same name. The berries are called *murtidda* in Sicilian.

mollica atturrata (Sic) toasted bread crumbs.

mollica di pane (Sic) bread crumbs. Another Sicilian word for bread crumbs is *muddica*. The Italian word is *pangrattato*.

montone (i) mutton.

monzù French chefs in Sicilian aristocratic families (from French *monsieur*).

mora (e) blackberry.

morbido soft.

moro type of blood orange. See *arance sanguinella*.

mortadella large pork sausage made of ground meat laced with cubes of fat.

moscardino (i) small octopus (*Eledone cirrosa*) with only one row of suckers on its arms.

moscato white grape used to make sweet dessert wines of the same name.

mosciame dried and pressed salted tuna.

mostarda mustard; also called *senape*. *Mostarda* in Sicily is also a paste made by boiling down freshly pressed grape juice or must (*mosto*).

mosto must; freshly pressed grape juice before fermentation.

mozzarella (e) fresh, soft cheese made from cow's milk.

muddica (Sic) bread crumbs. Also see *mollica di pane*.

muggine gray mullet (*Mugil cephalus*); also called *cefalo* (see *cefalo,* this *Guide*).

murena (e) moray eel (*Muraena helena*).

nasello (i) hake (*Merluccius merluccius*). Also called *merluzzo*.

neonata tiny, "newborn" fish such as whitebait, anchovy, sardine and herring served fried. Called *nunnata* in Sicilian.

nero black.

Nero d'Avola type of red grape used to make a variety of excellent wines.

nero di seppia cuttlefish ink and a black sauce made from it used to dress pasta.

nespola (e) medlar (*Mespilus germanica*). When the tart pulp becomes soft and ready to eat, the outer portion of the fruit begins to look rotten.

nocciola (e) hazelnut.

noccioline peanuts; also called *arachidi*.

noce (i) nut; walnut. Can also refer to a lean cut of beef or veal, such as *noce di vitello,* in an upscale restaurant.

noce di cocco coconut.

noce moscata nutmeg.

nocepesca (nocepesche) nectarine.

nodini di vitello veal medallions.

non fumatori no smoking.

non gassata not carbonated.

non troppo cotto cooked medium.

nostrale home-grown or locally grown. Also called *nostrano*.

novello fresh; tender.

nunnata (Sic) tiny, "newborn" fish. See *neonata*, this *Guide*.

oca (oche) goose.

occhiata (e) saddled bream (*Oblada melanura*).

odori aromatic herbs and vegetables used to flavor soups, sauces and stocks.

olio oil.

olio d'oliva olive oil.

olio di granturco corn oil.

olio di semi vegetable oil.

olio di semi di girasole sunflower oil.

oliva (e) olive. *Olivo* is olive tree (*Olea europea*).

olive al fiore tasty black olives with a very wrinkled surface.

olive bianche green olives.

olive nere black olives.

ombrina (e) fish (*Umbrina cirrosa*) similar to bass.

orata (e) gilthead bream (*Sparus aurata*).

orecchiette little ear-shaped pasta.

ortaggi greens.

orzo barley. The rice-shaped pasta that is called orzo in the United States is called *risoni* in Sicily. *Orzo perlato* is pearl barley.

osteria (e) traditionally a rustic eatery where wine and some basic food was served. Today it is often neither rustic nor inexpensive.

ostrica (ostriche) oyster (*Ostrea edulis*).

ovu ciurusu (Sic) soft-boiled egg. In Italian it is called *uovo a la coque*.

pagello (i) red porgy, a type of sea bream (*Sparus pagrus*).

pan carrè slice of American-style white bread.

pancetta cured pork belly.

pane (i) bread.

pane bianco white bread.

pane casareccio homemade or home-style bread.

pane di segale rye bread.

pane integrale whole-wheat bread.

pane rimacinate bread made from semolina flour.

pane tostato toast.

panetteria (e) bread bakery; also called *panificio*.

pangrattato bread crumbs. Sicilian terms for bread crumbs are *mollica di pane* and *muddica*.

panificio salumeria bakery that has expanded into a food shop.

panino (i) small roll; sandwich.

panino imbottito stuffed roll; sandwich. If American-style white bread is used, it is called a sandwich. A sandwich grilled in an electrical toaster is called a "toast." Ironically, Americans have come to know this as a *panini*.

panna heavy cream. Whipped cream is *panna montata*.

passata di pomodoro bottled puréed raw tomatoes.

passato purée; puréed.

passito sweet wine made with grapes partly dried in the sun to concentrate the sugars and flavor. *Passito* from the island of Pantelleria is highly regarded.

passoli dried currants.

passolina e pinoli mixture of small black currants and pine nuts.

pasta general term for food made from a dough of flour and water, sometimes with eggs. Pasta is made in many shapes and sizes. If the name of a pasta ends in *-ette* or *-ini,* it is the smaller version of the "regular" size. If it ends in *-oni,* it is a larger version of the "regular" size. *Pasta (e)* is also a word used for the small cakes sold in pastry shops. For example, *paste di mandorle* are almond cakes; *pasticcino* is a small cake.

pasta all'uovo pasta containing eggs.

pasta asciutta dried pasta, which is boiled and served with a sauce.

pasta d'acciuga anchovy paste.

pasta di mandorla marzipan; almond paste. See *pasta reale,* this *Guide.*

pasta filata see *formaggio a pasta filata,* this *Guide.*

pasta fresca fresh pasta (not dried); typically made from soft-wheat flour.

pasta frolla pastry crust.

pasta reale "royal paste"; marzipan, a mixture of sugar and ground almonds, which is often shaped and molded in imaginative ways. Marzipan fruits are called *frutta di martorana* because they are believed to have been invented by the nuns of the Martorana convent in Palermo. *Pasta reale* is used in a wide variety of sweets in Sicily. Also called *pasta di mandorla.*

pasta secca dried pasta, typically made from hard durum wheat.

pasta sfoglia thin sheet of pasta or pastry. Also called simply *sfoglia.*

pastella batter for frying.

pasticceria (e) pastry; pastry shop.

pasticcio (i) cake; pastry; pie. See *pasta,* this *Guide.*

pastina small pasta of various shapes, usually used in soup.

patata (e) potato.

patate bollite boiled potatoes. Also called *patate lesse.*

patate dolci sweet potatoes.

patate passate mashed potatoes. Also called *purée di patate* or simply *puré.*

patate saltate thinly sliced, sautéed potatoes.

FOODS & FLAVORS GUIDE

pecorino hard, sharp, sheep's milk cheese, which can be eaten with bread or grated. In Sicilian this cheese is named *picurinu*.

penne quill-shaped, tubular pasta. Small *penne* is *pennette;* ridged *penne* is *penne rigate*.

pepe pepper. *Pepe bianco* is white pepper; *pepe nero* is black pepper.

pepe di Caienna cayenne pepper.

pepe rosso paprika.

peperoncino (i) hot chile pepper.

peperone (i) bell pepper. A *peperone* may be *giallo* (yellow), *rosso* (red), or *verde* (green).

pera (e) pear.

perine very small and rare pears unique to Sicily.

pernice (i) partridge.

pesca (pesche) peach.

pesca tabacchiera somewhat flattened peaches with an indentation running from the top to the bottom and sweet, aromatic white or yellow flesh, grown on the slopes of Mt. Etna in the provinces of Catania and Messina.

pesca tardiva di Leonforte peach grown in Leonforte, covered with a paper bag throughout its development to ensure the production of an unblemished fruit without the use of pesticides.

pesce (i) fish.

pesce persico perch (*Perca fluviatilis*).

pesce San Pietro John Dory large-headed fish (*Zeus faber*) with tasty flesh.

pesce sciabola scabbard fish (*Lepidopus caudatus*), an eel-like fish. Also called *spatola*.

pesce spada swordfish.

pesce stocco (Sic) dried cod. See *baccalà,* this *Guide*.

pescheria (e) fish shop. *Pescheria* is also the name of the well-known, sprawling, open-air fish market in the oldest part of Catania.

pesciolini small fish such as whitebait.

pesto food ground to a paste. Also the name of a green sauce made with olive oil, crushed fresh basil leaves, pine nuts, garlic and grated pecorino cheese.

petto (i) breast. *Petto di manzo* is beef brisket; *petto di pollo* is chicken breast.

piadina soft, flat, round bread about 8 inches in diameter. It is grilled on an earthenware pan and is similar to pide bread.

piatti freddi cold dishes.

piatto (i) dish; plate; course at a meal.

piatto del giorno specialty of the day.

piatto fondo deep bowl used for the first course (*primo piatto*), which most frequently is a pasta preparation, but could also be a soup or rice dish.

piatto forte entrée; main course; also called *piatto principale* and, most commonly, *secondo piatto.*

piatto piano flat plate used for the main course (*secondo piatto*).

piatto principale main course; see *piatto forte.*

piatto unico a "one plate" meal in which the first course (*primo piatto*) and second course (*secondo piatto*) are served together. A *piatto unico* usually does not include pasta.

piccante spicy.

piccata (e) veal escallope. *Piccatina (e)* is a small veal escallope.

piccione (i) pigeon. Wild pigeon is *piccione selvatico.*

piccola colazione breakfast. *Prima colazione* and simply *colazione* also mean breakfast in Sicily, but in mainland Italy *colazione* means lunch.

piccolo small.

pinoli pine nuts.

pipittuna (Sic) large citron. *Cedro* is Italian for a citron of any size.

piselli peas.

pistacchio (i) pistachio nut.

pizza al taglio a square piece of pizza sliced from a larger, rectangular pizza, sold by weight in bakeries.

pizzetta (e) small pizza with a very thin crust.

polenta cooked cornmeal.

polipetto (i) baby octopus. See also *maiolini.*

polipo (i) octopus (*Octopus vulgaris*); also called *polpo (i).*

pollo (i) chicken. Spring chicken is *pollo novello.*

polmone lung.

polpa boneless beef; also means pulp, such as tomato pulp.

polpetta (e) meatball, unless otherwise specified.

polpo octopus; also called *polipo.*

pomodorino (i) di Pachino cherry tomato cultivated near the city of Pachino.

pomodoro (i) tomato.

pomodoro (i) secco (secchi) sun-dried tomato.

pompelmo (i) grapefruit. Pink grapefruit is *pompelmo rosa.*

popone (i) melon, more commonly called *melone.*

porcello (i) young pig. Suckling pigs are *porcellino (i)* or *maialino.*

porcini boletus wild mushroom (*Boletus edulis*) with a brown cap and barrel-shaped stem. In Sicily it usually is available only dried.

porro (i) leek.

pranzo lunch, the main meal of the day, eaten around 1:30 or 2 PM.

prezzemolo parsley.

prezzo (i) price. *Prezzo fisso* is fixed price.

prima colazione breakfast; *piccola colazione* and simply *colazione* also mean breakfast. The term *colazione* can mean lunch in the rest of Italy.

primo piatto first course, usually pasta, but can also be a soup or rice dish.

primosale "first salt"; slightly aged pecorino cheese made with sheep's milk that has been lightly salted.

prosciutto (i) aged, salt-cured, air-dried ham. It may be raw (*crudo*), cooked (*cotto*) or smoked (*affumicato*).

provola (e) globe- or pear-shaped cheese made from cow's milk. It is a type of *pasta filata* cheese. See *formaggio a pasta filata*.

provolone *pasta filata* cheese made from cow's milk. See *formaggio a pasta filata*.

provolone dolce young, smooth and mild provolone cheese.

provolone piccante sharp provolone cheese aged for six months to two years. It typically is used as a grating cheese.

prugna (e) plum; also called *susina*.

prugna secca (prugne secche) prune.

punte di asparagi asparagus tips.

punta di vitello veal brisket.

purea purée; also spelled *puré*.

quadrucci small, square-shaped pasta for soup.

quaglia (e) quail.

radicchio red-leafed chicory.

ragù chopped or ground meat slow-cooked in a frying pan, typically with celery, onions and carrots in olive oil.

ragusano brick-shaped *caciocavallo* cheese produced in Ragusa province. See *caciocavallo*.

rana pescatrice monkfish; angler fish (*Lophius spp*). Also called *coda di rospo*.

rapa (e) turnip.

ravanello (i) radish.

razza (e) skate; ray.

ribes currant. Black currant is *ribes neri;* red currant is *ribes rosso*.

ribes bianco gooseberry.

riccio (ricci) di mare sea urchin (*Paracentrotus lividus*). Also simply called *ricci*.

ricciola (e) amberjack (*Seriola dumerili*), a fish with a dark bluish-gray back and an amber stripe extending from cheek to tail along the midside of the body. Also called *aricciola*.

ricevuta (e) receipt; also called *fattura*.

ricotta fresh, soft sheep's or cow's milk cheese, made by heating the cheese-making by-product, whey, with more milk. Hence the name ricotta, meaning "recooked." Ricotta is often strained, sweetened and used in desserts.

ricotta infornata fresh ricotta cheese that is baked until lightly browned.

ricotta salata salted, dried ricotta used as a grating cheese.

rigaglie giblets. They are called *gisieri* in Sicily.

rigato ridged or ribbed (pasta).

rigatoni large, ribbed tubular pasta, one of the most common shapes of pasta.

ripieno (i) stuffing; also means stuffed.

riso rice.

riso integrale brown rice, rice with the bran but not the husk.

risoni rice-shaped pasta for soup; orzo.

ristorante (i) usually a more formal restaurant than a *trattoria* or *osteria*.

rognone (i) kidney.

rosatello rosé wine; also called *rosato* and, more commonly, simply rosé.

rosmarino rosemary. Wild rosemary is *rosmarino selvatico*.

rosso red.

rosticceria (e) snack bar selling hot and cold foods by weight. It can be on the same premises as a pastry shop and coffee bar. The food sold or eaten in these shop is also called *rosticceria*.

rucola arugula; also called *rughetta*.

salame (i) spicy, dry-cured pork sausage.

salame di cinghiale wild boar salami.

salame di maiale (suino) nero salami made from pork taken from black pigs in the Nebrodi Mountains. The large family of pork sausages that includes spicy, dry-cured varieties and soft or cooked varieties such as ham and mortadella are called *salumi di maiale (suino) nero dei Nebrodi*.

salamino piccante pepperoni.

salato salted or cured. It may refer to salt-cured meats.

sale salt.

salsa (e) sauce.

salsa di pomodoro tomato sauce. Also called *sugo di pomodoro*.

salsiccia (e) sausage.

saltato sautéed.

salumeria shop specializing in cured meat products. It can also be a shop selling all kinds of food. Also see *panificio salumeria,* this *Guide*.

salumi large family of pork sausages that includes spicy, dry-cured varieties and soft or cooked varieties such as ham and mortadella.

salvia sage.

salvietta napkin; also called *tovagliolo*.

sanguinello (i) type of blood orange. See *arancia sanguinella*.

sarago (saraghi) white bream (*Diplodus vulgaris,* also classified as *Diplodus sargus*).

sarda (e) sardine (*Sardinella anchovia*).

scalogna (e) shallot or scallion.

scaloppini (e) thin, pounded piece of meat; escallope.

scamorza cheese similar to but saltier than mozzarella.

scampo (i) prawn (*Nephrops norvegicus*).

scauzzi name of a medium-size land snail in southeastern Sicily. It is known in the rest of the island as *intuppateddi*. See *lumaca,* this *Guide.*

schiacciata (e) flat, rectangular or round loaf of bread. It may be cut in half and stuffed with cheese and ham.

sciroppo (i) syrup. *Sciroppato* is cooked in syrup.

scorfano (i) scorpion fish (*Scorpaena scrofa*).

secco dry.

secondo piatto second course, the main course; see *piatto forte*.

sedanini short, slightly curved tubular pasta resembling celery stalks.

sedano celery.

segale rye.

selvaggina game.

selvatico wild.

seme (i) seed.

semifreddo (i) semi-frozen dessert made with a base similar to *gelato* but with cream added. Compare with *gelato,* this *Guide.*

semplice plain.

senape mustard; also called *mostarda*.

senza without.

seppia (e) cuttlefish. *Seppioline* are small or baby cuttlefish.

servizio service; service charge.

servizio compreso service included. Another term for service included is *servizio incluso*.

servizio non compreso service not included. Another term for service not included is *servizio non incluso*.

sfoglia thin sheet of pastry or pasta. Also called *pasta sfoglia*.

sformato (i) dish such as quiche made in a baking pan.

sgombro (i) mackerel (*Scomber scombrus*).

soffritto "stir fried"; a mixture of chopped carrots, onions, garlic and celery sautéed in olive oil, the beginning step in the preparation of a variety of common Italian dishes, including soups and sauces.

sogliola (e) sole (*Solea vulgaris*).

soppressata firm salami made of chopped pork with black peppercorns, moistened with red wine. The salami is flattened during curing. *Soppressata* is also the name of a molded sausage of meat from pig's head in aspic.

sorbetto (i) sorbet.

sottaceti mixed pickled vegetables.

sott'olio preserved in olive oil, sometimes after pickling.

spaghetti tagliati spaghetti broken into small pieces, used for soups.

sparacelli Sicilian for broccoli.

spatola scabbard fish (*Lepidopus caudatus*).

specialità della casa specialty of the house.

specialità della zona local specialty. Also called *specialità locali*.

specialità di questo ristorante specialty of the restaurant.

speck smoked, dry-cured raw ham.

spezie spices.

spezzatino stew.

spicchio (i) d'aglio clove of garlic.

spiedo (i) spit; skewer. Spit-roasted foods are called *spiedini*.

spigola (e) sea bass (*Dicentrarchus labrax, Morone labrax*). Also called *branzino*.

spinaci spinach.

spremuta (e) freshly squeezed fruit juice.

spumante sparkling wine.

spuntino (i) snack.

stellette small star-shaped pasta used in soups.

stinco (stinchi) pork leg; shank.

stocco (Sic) dried cod. *Stocco* also is called *pesce stocco* and *stoccafisso*. Also see *baccalà*, or dried, salted cod, this *Guide*.

stracchino creamy, fresh cow's milk cheese typically eaten as a dessert cheese.

strapazzato scrambled.

strattu (Sic) concentrated, sun-dried tomato extract, called *estratto di pomodore*. See *estratto di pomodoro*, this *Guide*.

stuzzichino (i) appetizer; snack.

succo (succhi) juice. Fruit juice is *succo di frutta*.

sugo (sughi) juice; sauce; gravy.

sugo di pomodoro tomato sauce. Also called *salsa di pomodoro*.

suino pig; pork. Also called *maiale. Maiale* is a noun; *suino* is used either as a noun or as an adjective meaning pork.

suino nero dei Nebrodi Sicilian black pig of the Nebrodi Mountains, which grazes on acorns in the oak forests there. Its meat is highly prized.

susina (e) plum; also called *prugna.*

tacchino (i) turkey.

tagliatelle ribbon noodles about ¼-inch wide.

tagliato sliced; cut.

tagliolini fine cylindrical pasta similar to vermicelli, but shorter.

tarocco (tarocchi) type of blood orange. See *arancia sanguinella.*

tartaruga (tartarughe) turtle.

tartina (e) small, open-faced sandwich.

tartufo (i) truffle.

tasse incluse taxes included. Another way of noting this is *IVA incluse.*

tavola calda snack bar serving hot food.

tazza (e) cup.

tè tea. Iced tea is *tè freddo.*

tenero tender.

testa (e) head.

testa d'aglio head of garlic.

testa di vitello calf's head.

timo thyme.

tinca (tinche) tench (*Tinca tinca*), a freshwater fish.

tisana (e) herbal tea.

tonnato with tuna sauce.

tonno (i) tuna; called *tunnina* in Sicilian.

tortellini stuffed, ring-shaped pasta; a large version is called *tortellone (i).*

tortiglioni tubular pasta typically served with chunky sauces.

tostato toasted. Another word for toasted is *abbrustolito.*

totano (i) flying squid (*Todarodes sagittatus*).

tovagliolo (i) napkin. *Salvietta* is another word for napkin.

tramezzino (i) sandwich made with American-style white bread.

trancia (e) slice of fish.

trattoria (e) informal eatery.

trifolato (i) method of sautéeing vegetables in olive oil, garlic and parsley, which is used especially for cooking mushrooms.

triglia (e) red mullet (*Mullus barbatus*).

triglia (e) di scoglio striped red mullet (*Mullus surmuletus*).

trippa tripe. It is sold in butcher shops already boiled and cut into strips.

tritato ground; minced. Also means ground meat.

tritato di manzo ground beef. See *carne macinata,* this *Guide.*

trito minced or diced vegetables and herbs.

trota (e) trout.

tuma (Sic) very fresh, soft, mild, unsalted sheep's cheese.

tuorlo (i) yolk.

tutto compreso all-included.

uopa Sicilian name for the silvery bogue fish (*Boops boops*). Also called *vopa.*

uovo (a) egg.

uovo strapazzato scrambled egg.

uovo a la coque soft-boiled egg. In Sicilian it is called *ovu ciurusu.*

uovo al tegame fried egg.

uovo di tonno salted, pressed roe from tuna. Also called *bottarga di tonno.*

uovo sodo hard-boiled egg.

uva grape. *Uva bianca* is green grape; *uva nera* is black grape.

uva passa (uva passita) raisin; also called *uva secca.*

uva sultanina sultana; golden raisin.

vaccareddi (Sic) medium-size land snail. See *lumaca,* this *Guide.*

vaniglia vanilla.

vastedda (e) (Sic) sesame-topped soft bread bun. *Vastedda* also is the name of a fresh, flat, white sheep's cheese shaped like a bun, made in the Belice Valley. It also is another name for the cow spleen sandwich known more commonly as *focaccia con la milza* or *pane con la milza* (see *Menu Guide*).

ventresca underbelly of fish, especially of tuna, considered the most tender and tasty part of the fish.

ventriglio gizzard.

verde green.

verdello variety of highly aromatic green lemon.

verdura (e) green vegetable.

verdure amare local wild greens.

vergine pure grade of olive oil from the first cold pressing of fresh olives.

vietato fumare no smoking.

FOODS & FLAVORS GUIDE

vino (i) wine.

vino bianco white wine.

vino cotto grape juice boiled down to make a syrup.

vino da pasto table wine; also called *vino da tavola*.

vino rosatello rosè wine; also called *vino rosè*.

vino rosso red wine.

visciola wild sour morrello cherry used to make desserts and maraschino liqueur. Also called *marasca*.

vitello veal.

vongole clams. V*ongole veraci* or "true clams" (*Venerupis decussata*) have a darker shell and are reputed to have a better taste than golden-carpet clams, which are simply called *vongole*.

vopa (e) bogue fish (*Boops boops*). Also called *uopa*.

vurrania Sicilian word for borage. In Italian borage is called *borraggine*.

zafferano saffron.

zenzero ginger.

zibibbo variety of white grape typically grown on the island of Pantelleria. The naturally sweet *moscato* and *passito* wines are made from *zibibbo* grapes that have been sun-dried to concentrate their sugar and flavor.

ziti large tubular pasta similar to rigatoni, but without ridges.

zucca (zucche) pumpkin; gourd; squash. Also called *cucuzza,* the Sicilian term for all kinds of squash and zucchini.

zuccata preserves made from a bulgy type of zucchini called *zucchina centinara.* The preserves are white and nearly transparent. Cut in long thin strips, they are used to decorate cakes, especially *cassata*. See *Menu Guide.*

zucchero sugar.

zucchero a velo powdered sugar. Also called *zucchero in polvere*.

zucchina (e) zucchini.

zucchina (e) centenaria (e) variety of zucchini shaped like a large pear with pale green skin covered with green fuzz.

zucchina lunga Italian name for a variety of squash grown in Sicily. It is a long, smooth-skined, pale-green cylinder about two feet long.

zucchine pantesche oval, light green zucchini with dark green stripes, grown on the island of Pantelleria.

zuppa (e) soup. Also called *minestra*.

Restaurants

Chefs Who Taught Us Much about Sicilian Food

Al Fogher Ristorante, Contrada Bellia, Strada Statale 117 Bis, Piazza Armerina, Tel. 0935 684123, Angelo Treno, chef, alfogher@tin.it, www.alfogher.net

Antica Dolceria Bonajuto, Corso Umberto I, 159, Modica, Tel. 0932 941225, Franco Ruta and son, Pierpaolo, owners, info@bonajuto.it, www.bonajuto.it

Antica Stazione, Ficuzza, Tel. 091 8460000, Saverio Patti and Mariano Carbonetti, chefs, info@anticastazione.it, www.anticastazione.it

Corrado Costanzo, Via Spaventa, 7, Noto, Tel. 0931 835243, Giusy Costanzo, *pasticcere* and *gelatiere*

Fattoria delle Torri, Vico Napolitano, 14, Tel. 0932 751286, Modica, Peppe Barone, chef, peppebarone1960@libero.it

Hostaria Nangalarruni, Via delle Congraternite, 10, Castelbuono, Tel. 0921 671428, Giuseppe Carollo, chef, nangalaruni@libero.it, www.hostarianangalarruni.it

Il Vecchio Palmento Ristorante Pizzeria, Via Failla, 2, Castelbuono, Tel. 0921 672099, Lauro Francesco, chef

La Pasticceria di Maria Grammatico, Via Vittorio Emanuele, 14, Erice, Tel. 0923 869390, *pasticcere*

Locanda Don Serafino, Via Orfanotrofio, 39, Ragusa Ibla, Tel. 0932 248778, Vicenzo Candiano, chef, info@locandadonserafino.it, www.locandadonserafino.it

Osteria dei Vespri, Piazza Croce dei Vespri, 6, Palermo, Tel. 091 6171631, Alberto Rizzo, chef, osteriadeivespri@libero.it, www.osteriadeivespri.it

Ristorante Cin Cin, Via Manin, 22, Palermo, Tel. 091 6124095, Lucia Birrittella, chef, and son Vincenzo Clemente, who also is a chef, clemente.vincenzo@gmail.com, www.ristorantecincin.com

Ristorante Don Camillo, Via Maestranza, 96, Syracuse, Tel. 0931 67133, Giovanni Guarneri, chef, ristorantedoncamillo@tin.it, ristorantedoncamillosiracusa.it

Ristorante La Botte, Contrada da Lenzitti, 20, Monreale, Tel. 091 414051, Salvatore Cascino, chef, labotte@mauriziocascino.it, www.mauriziocascino.it

Ristorante La Pigna, Hotel Villa Paradiso dell'Etna, Via per Viagrande, 37, San Giovanni La Punta, Tel. 095 7512409, Giovanni Farruggio, chef

Ristorante Leon d'Oro, Viale Emporium, 102, San Leone, Tel./Fax: 0922 414400, Salvatore (Totò) and Vittorio Collura, owners, toto.collura@tin.it

Ristorante Monte San Giuliano, Vicolo S. Rocco, 7, Erice, Tel. 0923 869595, Matteo Giurlanda, chef, ristorante@montesangiuliano.it, www.montesangiuliano.it

Ristorante Ostaria del Duomo, Via Seminario, 5, Cefalù, Tel./Fax 0921 421838, Vincenzo Barranco, former chef, and sons, Davide, chef, and Allesio, maitre d'hotel, ostariadelduomo@libero.it, www.ostariadelduomo.it

Sicilia in Bocca Ristorante alla Marina, Via Dusmet, 35, Catania, Tel. 095 2500208, Gaetano Rapicavoli, chef, info@siciliainbocca.it, www.siciliainbocca.it

Trattoria il Delfino, Via Torretta, 80, Sferracavallo, Tel. 091 530282, Antonio Pedone and Antonio Billeci, co-owners, trattoriaildelfino@virgilio.it

Trattoria il Maestro del Brodo, Via Pannieri, 7, Palermo, Tel. 091 329523, Alissandro Arusa, chef, Bartolo Arusa, owner, giuseppearusa@libero.it

Bibliography

Benjamin, Sandra. *Sicily: Three Thousand Years of Human History*. Hanover, New Hampshire: Steerforth Press, 2006.

Bernabò Brea, Luigi. *Sicily Before the Greeks*. Norwich, England: Thames and Hudson, 1957.

Bugialli, Giuliano. *Foods of Sicily & Sardinia and the Smaller Islands*. New York: Rizzoli International Publications, Inc., 1996.

Cerchiai, Luca, Lorena Jannelli and Fausto Longo. *The Greek Cities of Magna Graecia and Sicily*. Los Angeles: The J. Paul Getty Museum, 2004.

Croce, Marcella and Moira F. Harris. *History on the Road: The Painted Carts of Sicily*. Lakeville, Minnesota: Pogo Press, 2006.

Dalby, Andrew. *Food in the Ancient World from A to Z*. London: Routledge, 2003.

Davidson, Alan. *Mediterranean Seafood*, 2nd edition. Baton Rouge, Louisiana: Louisiana State University Press, 1981.

Dickie, John. *Delizia! The Epic History of the Italians and Their Food*. New York: Free Press, 2008.

Edwards, John. *The Roman Cookery of Apicius: A Treasury of Gourmet Recipes & Herbal Cookery Translated and Adapted for the Modern Kitchen*. Point Roberts, Washington: Hartley & Marks, Publishers, 1984.

Finley, M.I. *Ancient Sicily*, revised edition. Totowa, New Jersey: Rowman and Littlefield, 1979.

Franzius, Enno. *History of the Byzantine Empire: Mother of Nations*. New York: Funk & Wagnalls, 1967.

Granof, Victoria. *Sweet Sicily: The Story of an Island and Her Pastries*. New York: HarperCollins, 2001.

Guido, Margaret. *Sicily: An Archaeological Guide*. London: Faber and Faber Ltd, 1967.

Holloway, R. Ross. *The Archaeology of Ancient Sicily*. London: Routledge, 1991.

Lanza, Anna Tasca. *The Flavors of Sicily: Stories, Traditions, and Recipes for Warm Weather Cooking*. New York: Clarkson Potter, Inc., 1996.

Leighton, Robert. *Sicily Before History: An Archaeological Survey from the Palaeolithic to the Iron Age*. Ithaca, New York: Cornell University Press, 1999.

Lowe, Alfonso. *The Barrier and the Bridge: Historic Sicily*. London: Geoffrey Bles, 1972.

Maggio, Theresa. *Mattanza: The Ancient Sicilian Ritual of Bluefin Tuna Fishing*. New York: Penguin Books, 2001.

Matthew, Donald. *The Norman Kingdom of Sicily*. Cambridge: Cambridge University Press, 1992.

Metcalfe, Alex. *Muslims and Christians in Norman Sicily: Arabic Speakers and the End of Islam*. London: RoutledgeCurzon, 2003.

Murray, Catherine Tripalin. *Grandmothers of Greenbush: Recipes and Memories of the Old Greenbush Neighborhood 1900–1925*. Madison, Wisconsin: Greenbush...remembered, 1996.

Olson, S. Douglas and Alexander Sens. *Archestratos of Gela: Greek Culture and Cuisine in the Fourth Century BCE*. New York: Oxford University Press, 2000.

Parasecoli, Fabio. *Food Culture in Italy*. Westport, Connecticut: Greenwood Press, 2004.

Prose, Francine. *Sicilian Odyssey*. Washington, DC: National Geographic Society, 2003.

Robb, John. *The Early Mediterranean Village: Agency, Material Culture, and Social Change in Neolithic Italy*. New York: Cambridge University Press, 2007.

Serventi, Silvano and Françoise Sabban. *Pasta: The Story of a Universal Food*. New York: Columbia University Press, 2002.

Simeti, Mary Taylor. *Pomp and Sustenance: Twenty-Five Centuries of Sicilian Food*. New York: Alfred A. Knopf, 1989.

Simonsohn, Shlomo. *The Jews in Sicily, Volume One, 383–1300*. Leiden, The Netherlands: Brill, 1997.

Smith, Denis Mack. *A History of Sicily: Ancient Sicily*. London: Chatto & Windus, 1968.

Smith, Denis Mack. *A History of Sicily: Medieval Sicily*. London: Chatto & Windus, 1968.

Smith, Denis Mack. *A History of Sicily: Modern Sicily After 1715*. London: Chatto & Windus, 1968.

Tornabene, Wanda and Giovanna, with Michele Evans. *Gangivecchio's Sicilian Kitchen*. New York: Alfred A. Knopf, 1996.

Tornabene, Wanda and Giovanna, with Michele Evans. *Sicilian Home Cooking: Family Recipes from Gangivecchio*. New York: Alfred A. Knopf, 2001.

Wilkins, John, David Harvey and Mike Dobson. *Food in Antiquity*. Exeter, England: University of Exeter Press, 1995.

Wilson, R.J.A. *Sicily under the Roman Empire: The Archaeology of a Roman Province, 36BC–AD535*. Warminster, England: Aris and Phillips Ltd, 1990.

Index

almond *mandorla* 2, 7, 10, 15, 26,
  28–29, 33, 36, 39, 82, 84, 86–88,
  91–94, 96, 99, 101–103, 106, 111,
  122–124, 127
amberjack *ricciola* 82, 112, 130
anchovy *acciuga* 38, 82, 88, 93, 97, 100,
  104, 109–112, 124–125, 127
anise *anice* 33, 112
apple *mela* 88, 124
apricot *albicocca* 8, 110
artichoke *carciofo* 8, 17, 21–22, 35, 62,
  71, 85–86, 90, 100, 103, 114–115,
  118, 120
  hearts *cuori di carciofi* 85, 118
  leaves *foglie* 62
asparagus *asparago* 24, 90, 112, 130

barley *orzo* 2–3, 126
basil *basilico* 97, 99, 111–112, 128
bay leaf *alloro* 9, 21, 87, 93, 111
bean *fagioli* (also see specific entries in
  English) 2, 5, 14, 20–21, 35–36,
  38, 89–90, 92–94, 97–98, 104,
  107–108, 114, 119–120, 123
beef *manzo; bue* 9, 21, 23, 38, 71,
  82–83, 86–87, 89, 91–93,
  100–102, 105, 111, 113–114,
  123–125, 128–129, 135
beer *birra* 30, 70, 113
beet *barbabietola; bietola* 112–113
biscuit *biscotto; galletta* 28–29, 33, 83,
  95, 106, 120
bluefish *pesce azzurro* 25

boar (wild) *cinghiali* 2, 23, 36–37, 98
  102–103, 116, 131
bogue fish *uopa* 101, 135–136
borage *borragine* 106–107, 113, 136
brain *cervello* 23, 87, 116
bread *pane* 2, 4, 8–9, 17, 19–20, 28, 30,
  33–34, 84–86, 88, 90–93, 96–101,
  103–104, 108, 116, 121, 124–128,
  132, 134–135
broccoli *spacarelli* 21–22, 84, 87, 97,
  113, 133
broth *brodo* 8, 32, 90, 113, 122
buckwheat *grano saraceno* 8, 121
butter *burro* 16, 22, 110–111, 114

cake *pasticcio* 6, 9, 28, 30, 33, 38, 84,
  86–92, 94–96, 102, 104, 107, 116,
  121, 127, 136
caper *cappero* 22, 37, 82, 84–85, 87–88,
  93, 96, 99, 105–107, 111, 115, 117
caper berries *cucunci* 37, 88, 96, 117
cardoon *cardo* 17, 86, 107, 115
carob *carruba* 8, 39, 89, 115
carrot *carota* 115
cauliflower *broccolo; cavolfiore* 21–22,
  48–49, 71, 84, 87, 97, 107, 113,
  115
celery *sedano* 132
cheese *formaggio* 4, 9, 19–20, 24–25,
  28, 30, 34–36, 39–40, 82–84,
  86–104, 106–108, 111, 114–115,
  120–121, 123–125, 128, 130–133,
  135

cherry *ciliegia* 27, 39, 81, 94, 98, 105, 111, 116, 123, 129, 136

chestnut *castagna* 27, 84, 86, 115

chicken *pollo* 3, 23–24, 55, 90–92, 100, 120, 128–129

chickpeas *ceci* 20, 33, 71, 82, 86, 88, 94, 96, 108, 115

chicory *cicoria* 116, 130

chocolate *cioccolata* 14–15, 28, 30, 38, 52, 83, 87, 89, 91–93, 95, 99, 102–104, 107, 116

cinnamon *cannella* 9, 15, 36–37, 85, 95, 99, 106, 114

citron *cedro* 26–27, 29, 87, 89, 98, 115, 129

citrus fruits *agrumi* (also see specific entries in English) 10, 17, 26–27, 110, 115, 123

clams *vongole* 105, 111, 114, 136

cloves *chiodi di garofano* 94–95, 116

cod (dried) 11, 85, 99, 105–106, 112, 128, 133

salted 83, 100, 106, 133

coffee *caffè* 27–29, 31, 81, 85, 92, 103, 112, 114, 131

corn *granoturco* 14, 36, 100, 119, 121, 123, 126

cornmeal *farina gialla* 36, 100, 119, 129

couscous *cuscus* 8–9, 32–33, 50, 89–90, 118

crab *granchio* 121

croissant *cornetto* 28, 87, 117

croquettes *crocchè* 82, 88, 117

cucumber *cetriolo* 116

cured pig's cheek *guanciale* 110, 121

currant *ribes* 9, 19, 22, 45, 82, 84–85, 88, 93, 97, 99, 101, 103–104, 108, 127, 130

custard *budino* 114

cuttlefish *seppia* 24–25, 47, 110, 125, 132

ink *nero di seppia* 25, 47, 110, 125

date *dattero* 5, 8, 24, 118

desserts (sweets) *dolci* 5, 9–10, 12, 22, 26–29, 33, 36–38, 64, 83, 85, 95, 98–99, 101–102, 106–107, 118, 121, 125, 127, 132–133

dill *aneto* 112

dolphin fish (mahi-mahi) *lampuga* 57, 122

drink (beverage) *bevanda* 30, 112–113

duck *anitra* 3, 23, 112

dumplings *gnocchi* 121

eel *anguilla* 24–25, 30, 38–39, 77–78, 80, 82, 112, 121–122, 125, 128

egg *uovo* 15, 38–39, 111, 113, 116, 120–121, 126, 135

white *bianco d'uovo* 111, 113, 116

yolk *giallo d'uovo* 69, 121, 135

eggplant *melanzana* 8, 15, 17, 19–21, 61, 63, 82, 85, 89, 93–94, 96–100, 103, 107, 111, 124

elderberry *bacca di sambuco* 112

endive *indivia* 43, 122

fava bean *fava* 2, 5, 20–21, 38, 46, 52, 63, 89–90, 93–94, 97, 104, 119–120, 123

fennel *finocchio* 21, 90, 92–93, 97, 100, 103, 119–120

wild *finocchietto* 90, 93, 97, 100, 103

fig *fico* 2, 26–28, 84, 103, 113, 116, 119

fish *pesce* (also see specific entries in English) 2, 4–5, 9–10, 19–20, 24–25, 32–33, 38–40, 71, 82–83, 85, 87, 89–90, 93, 95, 97, 101–105, 107–108, 111–112, 115–116, 118–119, 122, 124–126, 128, 130, 132–136

flour *farina* 2, 33–34, 36, 86–88, 96, 100, 102, 118–119, 121, 126–127

fritter *frittella* 33, 71, 82, 88, 96, 99, 104, 120

fruit *frutta* (also see specific entries in English) 3, 5, 8–10, 17, 24, 26–29, 37, 40, 71–72, 74, 79, 86, 88, 93–94, 96, 102, 109–110, 113–117, 119–120, 123, 125, 127–128, 133

game *selvaggina* 23, 114–115, 132
garlic *aglio* 20–21, 24, 110, 128,
   133–134
giblets *frattaglie* 120–121, 131
gizzard *ventriglio* 91, 135
goat *capra* 2, 22, 85, 98–99, 105, 115,
   123
goose *oca* 3, 16, 23, 126
grape *uva* 8–9, 17, 30, 33, 95, 105, 107,
   110, 121, 125, 127, 135–136
grapefruit *pompelmo* 26, 129
gray mullet *cefalo* 113, 116, 125
grouper *cernia* 87, 101, 116

ham *speck* 131, 133
   prosciutto 130
hazelnut *nocciola* 30, 87, 105, 125
heart *cuore* 29, 62, 118
herring *aringa* 92, 112, 125
honey *miele* 9, 28, 35, 39, 84, 88, 95,
   98–99, 106, 124
horse meat *carne di cavallo* 23, 115

ice cream *gelato* 29–30, 70, 84, 91, 96,
   103–105, 107, 116, 121, 132
ices *granite; sorbetto* 10, 29–30, 70, 88,
   91–92, 96, 103, 105, 110, 116,
   121, 123, 133

jams (jellies; preserves) *conserva* 9,
   27–29, 35, 38, 86–87, 89, 94, 96,
   116, 136
juice *succo* 9–10, 21, 24, 36, 82–83,
   86–87, 91, 95, 102, 110–111,
   121–122, 125, 133, 136

kidney *rognone* 23, 102, 114, 119, 131

lamb *agnello* 22–23, 82, 88, 95, 98,
   102, 105, 110, 117, 124
leek *porro* 53–54, 129
lemon *limone* 7, 21, 24, 26, 29, 31, 36,
   74, 82–83, 85–87, 91–92, 95,
   99–100, 102, 104, 106, 111, 115,
   122, 135

lentil *lenticchia* 2, 20, 35 108, 122
lettuce *lattuga* 43, 92, 122
lime *limetta* 26, 122
liqueur *liquore* 31, 33, 93, 104, 111,
   118, 122–124, 136
liver *fegato* 16, 23, 90, 92, 95–96, 105,
   119
lobster *aragosta* 32, 39, 54–55, 105,
   112
lung *polmone* 95–96, 129

mackerel *sgombro* 5, 25, 87, 133
mahi-mahi *lampuga* 57, 122
mandarin orange (tangarine) *mandarino*
   10, 70, 123
marzipan *pasta reale* 9, 28–29, 82, 86,
   95, 98, 102, 127
meat *carne* (also see specific entries in
   English) 8–9, 15, 19–24, 32,
   35–38, 56, 82–84, 86–87, 89–93,
   98–103, 105–106, 110–113, 115,
   122–125, 129–135
medlar *nespola* 26, 35
melon *melone* 8, 17, 27, 84, 109, 124,
   129
milk *latte* 23, 25, 30, 35–36, 39, 83, 85,
   88, 91, 93, 100–102, 113–115, 118,
   120, 122–125, 128, 130–131, 133
mint *menta* 21, 33, 85, 87, 94, 97, 102,
   106, 118, 124
mulberry *gelso* 7, 27, 29, 92, 121
mushroom *fongo* 37, 41–42, 87, 91,
   100, 111, 120, 129, 134
mussels *cozze* 43, 88, 92, 104, 108, 117

nougat *torrone* 36, 106–107
nut *noce* (also see specific entries in
   English) 9, 19, 22, 31, 45–46,
   48–50, 57, 60, 66–67, 82, 84–85,
   88, 93, 97, 99, 101–104, 106, 108,
   116, 125, 127–129
nutmeg *noce moscata* 15, 53, 100, 125

octopus *polpo* 15, 24, 61, 92–93, 95,
   100–101, 123, 125, 129

INDEX

oil *olio* 3, 19–22, 24, 30, 32, 82–89,
  91–106, 108, 110, 126, 128, 130,
  133–135
olive *oliva* 3, 17, 20–22, 24, 30, 32,
  82–89, 91–100, 102–111, 126,
  128, 130, 133–135
onion *cipolla* 9, 19–21, 33, 35, 82–83,
  85–87, 92–94, 98–99, 104–106,
  116, 130, 133
orange *arancia* 7, 10, 20, 26, 35, 37, 43,
  71, 82, 90, 92, 99, 112, 123, 125,
  132, 134
oregano *origano* 20–21, 33, 84, 86, 92,
  95, 98, 100, 102, 104

parsley *prezzemolo* 21, 24, 82–83,
  91–94, 99, 102, 105, 110–111,
  124, 129, 134
pasta *maccheroni* 8, 16, 19–20, 22,
  25–26, 33–34, 37–38, 40, 73,
  82–83, 86, 93–94, 96–99, 102,
  106–107, 110–116, 118–134, 136
peach *pesca* 10, 128
peanut *arachide* 112, 125
pear *pera* 14, 17, 25, 36, 114, 119, 128,
  130, 136
peas *piselli* 2, 21, 82, 90–91, 104–105,
  120, 129
pepper *pepe* 14, 20, 128
  bell pepper *peperone* 14, 21, 87, 128
  chile pepper *peperoncino* 14, 111, 128
persimmon *cachi* 27, 114, 123
pine nuts *pinoli* 9, 19, 22, 82, 84–85,
  88, 93, 97, 99, 101, 103–104, 108,
  127–129
pistachio *pistacchio* 7, 20, 25, 30, 38,
  45, 47, 83–84, 89–91, 98–99, 129
pork *suino* 2, 22–23, 37–38, 83, 88–90,
  93, 101, 103, 105–106, 108, 110,
  112–113, 115–117, 123, 125–126,
  129, 131–134
  black pig *suino nero dei Nebrodi* 23,
    37, 52, 90, 93, 131, 134
potato *patata* 14, 17, 22, 34, 82–83,
  86–88, 90–92, 98, 100, 104–105,

119, 121, 127
prickly pear *fico d'India* 14, 17, 27, 36,
  119
pudding *budino* 69, 83, 88, 91, 114

quail *quaglia* 94, 130
quince *cotogna* 88, 117, 124

rabbit *coniglio* 23, 87, 89, 116
raisin *uva passa* 103, 135
red mullet *triglia* 107, 135
rice *riso* 8, 11, 19–20, 34, 42, 51,
  55–56, 82, 102, 122, 126, 128,
  130–131
ricotta *ricotta* 9, 20, 24–26, 28, 33–36,
  39–40, 66–67, 83, 85–86, 88–92,
  94–98, 101–102, 104, 106, 111, 131
ricotta cream *crema di ricotta* 9, 28, 33,
  67, 85–86, 94, 102, 106
rosemary *rosmarino* 21, 60–61, 98, 124,
  131

saffron *zafferano* 21–22, 36, 82–83,
  97–98, 136
sage *salvia* 107, 124, 132
salad *insalata* 21, 26, 92, 110, 122
salami *salame* 23, 35, 37, 59–60, 88, 92,
  98, 102–103, 122, 125, 131, 133
salt *sale* 3, 131
sardines *sarde* 25, 33, 49–50, 97,
  100–101, 103, 113, 125, 132
sauce (gravy; juice) *sugo* 20, 133
scabbard fish *pesce sciabola* 93, 103,
  105, 128, 133
scallion *cipolla scalogna* 92, 116, 132
scorpion fish *scorfano* 103, 132
sea bass *spigola* 105, 113, 133
sea urchins *ricci* 25, 71, 105, 130
sesame seed *cimino* 83, 88, 92, 102,
  116
shallot *scalogna* 43, 132
shrimp *gambero* 24, 43, 85, 90–91, 97,
  120–121, 132
snails, land *lumache* 21, 34, 83, 93,
  108, 112, 117, 119, 123, 132, 135

soup *minestra* 5, 20, 30, 34, 38, 110,
   123–124, 126–128, 130–131, 133,
   136
spinach *spinaci* 24, 43, 82, 90–91, 102,
   104, 106, 133
spleen *milza* 33, 71, 95–96, 101, 124,
   135
squash *zucca* 14, 21, 71, 90, 108, 117,
   136
squid *calamari* 24, 47–48, 84–85, 90,
   103–105, 107, 110, 114, 134
stew *spezzatino* 8, 82, 84, 93, 95, 100,
   103, 105, 108, 133
strawberry *fragola* 29, 35, 117, 120
string bean *fagiolini* 24, 119
sugar *zucchero* 7, 9, 11, 12, 14–15, 26,
   35, 39, 127, 136
swordfish *pesce spada* 20, 25, 36,
   85–86, 93, 97, 99, 128
syrup *sciroppo* 27, 39, 65–67, 70, 132,
   136

tea *tè* 134
tomato *pompodoro* 14–15, 17, 20–21,
   35, 39, 110–111, 116, 118–119,
   127, 129, 131, 133
tomato extract (sun-dried) *estratto di
   pomodoro* 97, 133
tomato sauce *salsa di pomodoro* 20,
   110, 118, 131, 133
tongue *lingua* 93, 99, 122
tripe *trippa* 23, 107, 135
tuna *tonno* 2, 5, 10, 12, 14, 25, 32, 36,
   86–87, 101, 104, 106–107, 113,
   122, 125, 134–135
   salted, pressed roe *bottarga* 32, 85,
      104, 113, 135

veal *vitello* 9, 23, 56–57, 86, 93, 107,
   117, 120, 125, 129, 130, 136
vegetables *verdure* (also see specific
   entries in English) 3, 5, 8, 19–22,
   24, 26, 32, 40, 72, 74, 79, 82–83,
   87, 89–90, 92, 103, 107, 109, 113,
   116, 121, 123, 126, 135

wild *verdure amare* 21, 24, 90, 103,
   106–107, 135
vinegar *aceto* 21, 110, 115

water *acqua* 7–8, 10, 30, 110
watermelon *anguria* 27, 91, 124
wheat *frumento* 2–5, 8, 13–14, 17, 19,
   30, 33–34, 88, 96, 118–121,
   126–127
   durum wheat *farina rimacinata* 8,
      96, 119, 121, 127
white bream *sarago* 103, 132
wine *vino* 3, 8–9, 17, 28, 30–31, 33–34,
   37, 114, 118, 122–123, 125–127,
   131, 133, 136

zucchini *zucchina* 9, 20–21, 28, 44, 86,
   89, 90, 94, 96–98, 108, 117, 120,
   136

design   Ekeby
cover design   Susan P. Chwae
color separations   Traver Graphics, Inc.
printing   Sheridan Books, Inc.

typefaces   Garamond Simoncini and Helvetica Black
paper   60# Offset